Armstrong

Armstrong

David Bradbury

HAUS PUBLISHING · LONDON

First published in Great Britain in 2003 by
Haus Publishing
26 Cadogan Court, Draycott Avenue
London SW3 3BX

Copyright © David Bradbury 2003

The moral right of the author has been asserted

A CIP catalogue record of this work is available from the British Library

ISBN 1-904341-46-2 (paperback)
ISBN 1-904341-47-0 (hardback)

Typeset by Palimpsest Book Production Limited,
Polmont, Stirlingshire

Printed and bound by Graphicom in Vicenza, Italy

Cover Image: photograph of Louis Armstrong courtesy of Hachedé
Back cover: painting of Louis Armstrong by Trog

CONTENTS

In memory of

John Kendall
Ray Bolden
Ken Gallacher
Arvell Shaw

Coal Cart Blues

Louis Armstrong was the dominant figure in the newly conceived art of jazz, an entertainer who won the unstinting and enduring love of a global audience, and the hero of an American epic. He was also a willing and inventive participant in the creation of his own myth.

Armstrong celebrated his birthday as 4 July 1900. It was only after his death that a certificate was discovered which showed that in fact he had been born on 4 August 1901, and that three weeks later he was christened at the Sacred Heart of Jesus Roman Catholic church on South Lopez Street in New Orleans. Father J M Toomey, in the Latin used by Catholic priests at the time, described him on the certificate as 'niger, illegitimus'.

The illegitimate black boy was named Louis – not Louis Daniel, a name he is sometimes awarded in reference books – and he pronounced it 'Lewis', although he was also known in his younger days as Little Louie, and later as Pops, Dippermouth, Satchelmouth, Satchmo or Satch.

His mother was no more than 16 years old, born in a country town outside New Orleans as Mary Ann Miles, but affectionately known to her son as Mayann. His father was Willie Armstrong, a powerful and determined man with a steady job, but also with another family, for which he deserted Mayann about the time Louis was born.

He spent his first years in one of the poorest neighbourhoods in a city where luxury and squalor lived side by side, in his grandmother's single-storey house in Jane Alley, also called James Alley, which ran between Gravier and Perdido Streets in the neighbourhood known as Back o'Town, near the corner of present-day Tulane Avenue and Broad Street, about two miles from the levee keeping the waters of the Mississippi River at bay. The nearest landmark was the House of Detention, where short-term prisoners spent their nights, while their days were occupied in sweeping away the filth that collected in the city's markets, work so unpleasant that it earned them eleven days' remission on a 30-day sentence. In 'Buddy Bolden's Blues', named after one of the founding heroes of New Orleans jazz, Jelly Roll Morton sang:

> *I thought I heard Judge Fogarty say:*
> *'Thirty days in the market, take him away,*
> *Give him a good broom, take the pris'ner away,'*
> *I thought I heard him say.*[1]

The slum where Louis was born had a tough reputation; *Mayann told me that the night I was born there was a great big*

New Orleans, the Crescent City built along a bend on the Mississippi's left bank, stands on a swamp. Mark Twain, who knew it as a steamboat pilot, wrote that with the river in flood 'the water is up to the enclosing levee rim, the flat country lies low – representing the bottom of a dish – and as the boat swims along, high on the flood, one looks down upon the houses and into the upper windows. There is nothing but that frail breastwork of earth between the people and destruction.'[2]

Founded by the French in 1715, New Orleans had prospered, after Louisiana became part of the United States, as a port leading to the heartland of America by the great river system. But the Civil War cut it off, and the growth of railways damaged its economic importance.

Canal Street split the city in two: east of Canal was Downtown, the French section, where descendants of the original settlers shared with their black servants a European culture; west of Canal was Uptown, the American city, its English-speaking black people poorer, and less well-educated.

shooting scrape in the Alley, and two guys killed each other,[3] Armstrong recalled later. *In the alley more people were crowded than you ever saw in your life. There were churchpeople, gamblers, hustlers, cheap pimps, thieves, prostitutes and lots of children. There were bars, honky-tonks and saloons, and lots of women walking the streets for tricks to take to their 'pads', as they called their rooms.*[4] Mayann moved away, to a neighbourhood nearer to the river at Liberty and Perdido Streets, notorious for drink and prostitution: *Whether my mother did any hustling I cannot say.* Willie got a job near Jane Alley, a hot, smelly job stoking the fires to sweat turpentine out of pine logs. *From the time my parents separated I did not see my father again until I had grown to a pretty good size, and I did not see Mayann for a long time either.*[5]

The infant Armstrong was left with his grandmother, Josephine Armstrong, who earned her living by taking in white families' laundry. *Ever since I was a baby I have had a great love for my grandmother. She spent the best of her days raising me and teaching me right from wrong.*[6] She sent him to school, taught him *how to take care of myself, how to wash myself and brush my teeth, put my clothes away, mind the older folks,*[7] and reinforced her lessons with a stick. She took him to church: *In church and Sunday school I did a whole lot of singing. That, I guess, is how I acquired my singing tactics.*

Armstrong at 17, with his sister and their mother, Mayann

New Orleans was a complex racial and social web. French-speaking descendants of early settlers called themselves creoles, meaning that they had been born abroad. 'The common assumption that creole connotes Negro blood is bitterly resented,'[10] H L Mencken wrote as late as 1945. But there were large numbers of 'creoles of colour' because creole men found mistresses among their slaves or young women of mixed race. Children of these liaisons were often freed from slavery to find comfortable niches in skilled work, commerce and even cotton planting. They were classified into mulattos, quadroons or octoroons, depending on the proportion of African parentage. But in 1894 Louisiana Legislative Code No. 111 declared that a person with any African ancestry was black. The creoles of colour were suddenly equal with the people they despised, the English-speaking blacks lately freed from slavery who had moved to the city from the plantations.

In the meantime Mayann and Willie got together again, then split up. Mayann was left with another baby, a girl named Beatrice. *I did not see her until I was five years old,*[8] wrote Armstrong. His mother was ill and sent for him to look after the baby. With one of his mother's friends, he travelled on a tramcar for the first time. Nearly fifty years later he was to remember how shocked the woman was when he innocently sat in a seat at the front of the car instead of one marked FOR COLORED PASSENGERS ONLY. *There is something funny about those signs on the street cars in New Orleans. We colored folks used to get real kicks out of them when we got on a car at the picnic grounds or at Canal Street on a Sunday evening when we outnumbered the white folks. Automatically we took the whole car over, sitting as far up front as we wanted to. It felt good to sit up there once in a while. We felt a little more important than usual.*[9]

Mayann soon recovered from her illness and went back to work, as a domestic servant. Louis and his sister, nicknamed Mama Lucy, went scavenging *among those produce places where they used to throw away spoiled potatoes and onions into a big barrel. And she & I among other kids used to raid those barrels, cut off the spoiled parts and sell them to restaurants. There was a baker shop that used to sell two loaves of stale (the day after baked) bread for a nickel. They would do that to help the poor children.*[11] In the room they shared with their mother they met a series of 'stepfathers'; one they liked was Tom Lee, a chef at a Downtown hotel who brought home the white guests' leftovers. *Mama Lucy and I slept on a pallet on the floor nicely padded. That gave Mayann and Tom the whole bed for themselves. We both had gotten old enough to know when Mayann and Tom were getting a little nookie.*[12]

By the age of seven Armstrong was at work himself when he wasn't at school, helping a family of Russian Jewish immigrants called Karnovsky who had started a rag-and-bone business from their yard at Girod and Franklin Streets with two horses and two carts, later diversifying into coal deliveries. At night Louis would help young Morris Karnovsky deliver buckets of coal to prostitutes' cribs in the red-light district, Storyville; in the day he would help with the rag-and-bone collections. To tell people the cart was coming he had to blow on a tin horn. When he removed the wooden mouthpiece from the horn, he discovered that by blowing through his fingers he could get a tune out of it. He was already exposed to the music of the city, the bands that paraded through the streets for a funeral or were hauled along on wagons to advertise a picnic on Lake Pontchartrain, a streetcar ride to the north. He was 'second lining', joining the group of fans who marched and danced along, particularly when the band was led by the cornet-player Joe Oliver. *As long as he was blowing that was who I wanted to hear at any chance that I'd get.*[13] Oliver became a lifelong hero.

The Karnovsky family kept reminding me that I had talent – perfect tonation when I would sing. One day I was on the wagon with Morris Karnovsky: we were on Rampart and Perdido Streets and we passed a pawn shop which had in its window an old tarnished beat-up

B-flat cornet. It only cost five dollars. Morris advanced me two dollars on my salary. Then I put away 50 cents each week from my small pay – finally the cornet was paid for in full. Boy, was I a happy kid.[14]

That was how Armstrong remembered it in 1969, as he lay recuperating at the Beth Israel Hospital in New York City, in a hand-written 78-page manuscript that was his third major attempt at an autobiography. It is part of a long reminiscence about the Karnovskys and their generosity in employing and feeding him, bitterly comparing the behaviour of Jewish people in general with that of African Americans, and praising Jews for their food, their energy, their music and above all for their ability to stick together in adversity.

We know so much about Armstrong's youth because he wrote about it, in letters, magazine articles and books. Writing – he called it typing – was his main leisure pursuit. But his accounts of events often contradict each other: not everything he wrote can be taken literally, and the passage about the Karnovskys is an example. In it Armstrong repeatedly refers to the family's getting together in 1907 to sing 'A Russian Lullaby', and he quotes the lyrics. So there can be no doubt that he means the song of which Irving Berlin's daughter wrote that in '1927 my father seems to have written just one song – a great one – "Russian Lullaby"'.[15] Armstrong's memory might have been wrong in other details as well, after a serious illness at the age of nearly 70. And although it is certain that he had begun to be keenly interested in music, had formed a barber-shop quartet with friends to sing on street corners, and that his fellow musicians Sidney Bechet and Bunk Johnson remembered him as a kid with a cornet, it is still possible that the traditional story is correct, and that he did not pick up the instrument until after he fell into the hands of the police in the early hours of New Year's Day, 1913.

As Louis and his pals strolled down South Rampart Street among the New Year crowds, hoping to earn a few cents from their songs, another boy fired off six blanks from a pistol – not an uncommon contribution to the fireworks, noise and music. Tucked in his shirt, Louis had a .38 revolver that he had found in Mayann's trunk: it belonged to one of his 'stepfathers'. Cheered on by his friends, he pulled it out and fired it into the air. *A minute or so after I shot off that old gun, an old grey-haired detective came up behind me and hugged me and said: 'You're under arrest!'*[16]

The policeman, Edward Holyland, took his prisoner to the juvenile court building on Baronne Street and, after spending the rest of the night alone in a cell, he appeared before Judge Andrew H Wilson, the head of the court. By the end of the morning, he was in a horse-drawn Black Maria on his way to the Colored Waif's Home for Boys, on a tract of swampy farmland at the edge of the city. He was sent there for an indefinite period, and seems to have had trouble with the law before, perhaps for stealing newspapers to sell. The New Orleans daily paper, the *Times-Picayune*, said in its report of New Year disorder by youngsters: 'The most serious case was that of Louis Armstrong, a twelve-year-old negro, who discharged a revolver at Rampart and Perdido Streets. Being an old offender he was sent to the negro Waif's Home.'[17]

He summed it up later as a *boy's jail*.[18] But the Waifs' Home was an enlightened social innovation when he was sent there. Although there had been for some years an institution for young white offenders, black boys in trouble were simply sent to a black adult prison. In 1906 the Colored Branch of the Society for the Prevention of Cruelty to Children, using a derelict two-storey building, opened the Waifs' Home under the direction of Joseph Jones, a black ex-soldier who set out to give a fresh start to boys who had often been living impoverished existences on the streets. Food and conditions were spartan, from a lack of funds rather than a plan for punishment, though Armstrong saw a returned runaway given 105 lashes.[19] The hundred or

Armstrong (arrowed) in the 'Colored Waif's Home' band

more boys were taught reading, writing and arithmetic, and worked in the garden. Captain Jones, as he was known, disciplined them as if they were little soldiers, drilling them with dummy rifles and insisting on barrack-room standards of cleanliness. They went to bed, woke up and ran to meals at the sound of the bugle.

There was also a 15-piece brass band – a term Americans use to include bands with reed instruments such as clarinets and saxophones. Its conductor and trainer was Peter Davis, who had a deep-rooted suspicion of Armstrong and the rough neighbourhood he came from. But he started singing lessons and after about six months Davis relented and invited him to a band rehearsal. Armstrong was disappointed to be handed a tambourine instead of the cornet he wanted. *But I did not say a word. Taking the tambourine, I started to whip it in rhythm with the band. Mr Davis was so impressed he immediately changed me to the drums. He must have sensed that I had the beat he was looking for.*[20] After a successful performance on the drums, he was next handed an alto horn – in British band parlance a tenor horn, a three-valve instrument in the upright shape of a miniature tuba, made for playing the middle parts of arrangements; as Armstrong wrote: *I had been singing for a number of years and my instinct told me that an alto takes a part in a band as a baritone or tenor in a quartet. I played my part on the alto very well.*

Davis began to encourage him and his confidence grew as he felt that his admired teacher liked him: *As time went on I commenced being the most popular boy in the Home. Seeing how much Mr Davis liked me and the amount of time he gave me, the boys began to warm up to me.*[21] When the Home's bugler was allowed to leave, Louis took his place, polished up the *old filthy green* bugle, and began to *blow real mellow tones. The whole place seemed to change. Satisfied with my tone, Mr Davis gave me a cornet and taught me how to play 'Home Sweet Home'. Then I was in seventh heaven. Unless I was dreaming, my ambition had been realised.*[22]

Soon, Davis appointed Armstrong leader of the band and he was able to parade with it through his old neighbourhood, where, he said, the pimps and hustlers threw enough money into the hat for the band to buy new instruments and uniforms. Finally, after about eighteen months, he was allowed home: although he gave several different accounts of what happened, the probability is that he was released into the custody of his respectable father and his growing second family, but soon moved back to live with Mayann. The young cornet player began to play in parks and parades: bandleaders were encouraged to let him join in by his friend, 'Black Benny' Williams, who was a first-class bass-drummer.

On 8 August 1915, Armstrong's cousin, Flora Miles, gave birth to a baby, named Clarence. An older white man was suspected of being the father, but the family felt helpless to force him to take any responsibility, so young Louis began to look after Clarence himself, and unofficially adopted him when Flora died soon afterwards. To support Clarence, Mayann, Mama Lucy and himself, Armstrong took another job on a coal cart, hard work that nevertheless left his nights free to use his talent as a musician in his neighbourhood.

Armstrong lived where the black working men from the steamboats and the levees came to find gambling, booze and prostitutes. There were dance halls where the band had to play out of reach of the customers, from a balcony a dozen feet above the dance floor. One of them, at 1319 Perdido Street, was the Union Sons Hall, or Kenna's, better known as Funky Butt Hall. Armstrong claimed to have stood outside it and heard the legendary Buddy Bolden play there, though by 1907 drink and syphilis had put Bolden into the East Louisiana State Hospital, where he died in 1931. On every corner there were honky-tonks, cheap saloons with rooms above where a man could take

The fusion of African and European music which is jazz was encouraged in New Orleans by the presence of two cultures side by side. Until the 1870s slaves were allowed to meet in the eastern part of the city. Sidney Bechet, the great clarinet and saxophone player, recalled what his grandfather told him: 'Sundays when the slaves would meet – that was their free day – he beat out rhythms on drums at the square – Congo Square they called it – and they'd all be gathered there around him.'[23]

The city loved all kinds of music, and a dance-band player, black or white, might also be a member of a symphony orchestra. But when Armstrong was a boy the music in the streets and dance halls was not jazz. A Downtown band, made up of skilled readers, might play 'a dance set of waltzes, schottisches, polkas and two-steps, ending with a quadrille and a march to the refreshment counter'.[24] Gradually ragtime entered the repertoire though the rougher Uptown bands, and the cornet player Buddy Bolden is traditionally credited with introducing the 'hot blues', based on a folk-song form developed by slaves.

a prostitute, and rooms behind where he could gamble away his pay. Jelly Roll Morton said: 'These honky-tonks ran wide open twenty-four hours a day and it was nothing for a man to be drug out of one of them dead. Their attendance was some of the lowest-calibre women in the world, and their intake was the revenue from the little, pitiful gambling games they operated, waiting for a sucker to come in.'[25]

Armstrong lived in a neighbourhood called 'the Battleground', now demolished and partly replaced by City Hall and the huge Superdome football stadium; It was a short walk to the edge of what musicians knew as the District, but jazz history records as 'Storyville', a memorial to a politician called Alderman Sidney Story. He pushed through, despite fierce opposition in a city in which income from prostitution was second only to the income from the port, Section I of Ordinance 13,032 CS. Under it the Common Council of New Orleans marked out an area outside which 'it shall be unlawful for any prostitute or woman notoriously abandoned to lewdness, to occupy, inhabit, live or sleep in any house, room or closet.'[26] Story's aim was a forerunner of the English Street Offences Act 1959, an attempt to sweep prostitution out of the sight of respectable citizens. The District came into existence on 1 October 1897.

Approximately 2,000 prostitutes were registered for work in the District, a highly organised zone for male entertainment which published a Blue Book listing the women and advertising the brothels, at the pinnacle of which were the thirty or so luxurious palaces run by the leading madames, including Lulu White, Josie Arlington, Bertha Weinthal and Gipsy Shaeffer. In the strata below these elegant 'sporting houses' were cafés, dance halls, cabarets, casinos – all of them segregated for the use of whites. *The Negroes were only allowed to work in the Red Light District. As far as buy a little trim – that was absolutely out of the question,*[27] Armstrong recalled, and although there was plenty of work for musicians, dark-skinned men like him were barred from the best-paying jobs, such as playing solo piano at Lulu White's Mahogany Hall. That was Jelly Roll Morton's job: *They had lots of players in the District that could play lots better than Jelly, but their dark colour kept them from getting the job. Jelly Roll made so much money in tips that he had a diamond inserted in one of his teeth. No matter how much his diamond sparkled, he still had to eat in the kitchen, the same as we blacks.*[28]

Armstrong himself had a job as a musician at Henry Ponce's honky-tonk, playing the blues for the prostitutes. In fact, the blues was most of what he could play at the time, but he continued to improve under Joe Oliver's guidance. *I often did errands for Stella Oliver, his wife, and Joe would give me lessons for my pay.*[29] He also gave Armstrong one of his old cornets, and when Armstrong's girlfriend was sick and he needed money to pay the doctor, Oliver sent him to deputise for him in the band at Pete Lala's saloon on Customhouse Street. Meanwhile Armstrong was practising, and playing with his own band of youngsters modelled on the one Oliver led with the trombonist Kid Ory.

'At that time I saw a lot of Louis; I liked him fine. He was a good musicianer.'

–Sidney Bechet[30]

The twenty-year existence of 'Storyville' ended on 12 November 1917. The United States had entered the First World War and thousands of troops were passing through New Orleans to embark for Europe. After the deaths of four sailors in the District earlier in the year the Mayor of New Orleans reluctantly bowed to the demands of the Navy and outlawed brothels throughout the city. How catastrophic the change was to musicians, waiters and prostitutes is open to question. 'Work did gradually get scarcer, of course, so there was an exodus, but it was not a mass movement. And as for vice, well, much as the earlier effort to close the Storyville section had been a partial failure, so the effort to stamp it out was only an apparent success. Whoring and drinking simply went underground or moved out of the District and became a little less brassy and overt.'[31]

Armstrong's home life altered. Playing a dance out of town in a honky-tonk he later rated as the toughest place he ever worked, he fell for a skinny prostitute named Daisy Parker, three years older than him and living with a drummer. They married and found an apartment. Armstrong discovered that her idea of love was *to beat the hell out of her every night and make love in order to get some sleep . . . She was so mean and jealous. And to my surprise I awakened one morning and Daisy had a big bread knife laying on my throat, with tears dropping from her eyes, saying, 'You black son-of-a-bitch, I ought to cut your God-damn throat.*[32] Perhaps in an effort to stabilise the relationship, he brought Clarence, by then a three-year-old toddler, to live with them. One rainy day, Clarence was playing by himself on a porch overlooking the back yard when he slipped and fell on his head. He got up and climbed the steps, crying. *We ran to him immediately to see if he was hurt, rushed him to a doctor . . . All the doctors said the fall had set Clarence back four years behind the average normal child.*[33] Armstrong looked after the partially disabled Clarence from then on. He soon left Daisy and took Clarence back to Mayann with him.

Armstrong was one of the party that gathered to see off Joe Oliver in the summer of 1918 when he got an offer to work in Chicago. As Oliver's train steamed out, Kid Ory asked him to take Joe's place in the band, the hottest in town. *Yea I was a proud young man, playing in Kid Ory's band.*[34] Armstrong had followed the band so closely that he knew the repertoire, and joining Ory meant steady work, because the band was popular enough for Ory to be able to promote his own dances on Mondays, the usual day off. When there was a funeral or a parade, Armstrong was being asked to play with the Tuxedo Brass Band, the premier marching band led by Oscar 'Papa' Celestin. The First World War was over and so was the danger of being drafted into the army, so Armstrong was able to give up his respectable day job on the coal cart and turn to music full time. Parted from Daisy, he could take jobs wherever he chose, and his next move was on to the Mississippi.

Armstrong's first trip on a riverboat showed him a way of life more decorous and disciplined than the one he had known in the District. Captain John Streckfus and his four sons were determined that their boats should be well-oiled machines for separating people from their money without causing them any anxiety, much in the way Las Vegas does today.

The Streckfus Steamboat Line owned three or four boats at different times – steamboats had a way of catching fire or grounding on a sandbar – and its base was at St Louis, a thousand miles upriver from New Orleans. The bass-player Pops Foster, who worked alongside Armstrong, said that they carried no passengers or cargo, but simply took people on excursions up and down the river, with dancing in ballrooms on the upper deck where the cabins were on other boats. During the summer a boat might 'tramp' as far north as Dubuque, Iowa, mooring at small towns along the way to take passengers on evening cruises: it would return to St Louis by the end of May and then move down river to New Orleans for the winter. Some boats had white bands, some black, but all the patrons were white except for Monday night trips from St Louis and some other northern ports. 'We called Mondays "Getaway Night" because you could get away with anything,' said Foster. 'The guys in the band would walk around smoking cigarettes and drinking, and come down off the stand.'[35] The Streckfuses emphasised food rather than drink, but when Prohibition began, bootleggers sold whiskey out of the iceboxes meant for ice-cream and soda pop.

Fate Marable was the ideal bandmaster for the enterprise – he joined the line in 1907 and retired in 1940. The talent which had won Marable the trust of the Streckfus family was his skill at the keyboard of the steam calliope, a set of organ pipes given a powerful voice by the boat's boiler, to bring people hurrying to the landing stage while the steamboat itself was still out of sight around the bend. But Marable's ability went beyond taming the unwieldy instrument: he was also a well-schooled pianist and arranger ready to turn his hand to making the ship's band live up to the Streckfus Line's exacting demands, which one of the brothers, Captain Joe, would enforce with a stopwatch.[36]

Marable did not record until after Armstrong left, but his only two sides give an idea of the sort of music that was sent echoing over the Mississippi. On 'Frankie and Johnny' a pompous fanfare leads into an orchestral version of the familiar ballad interrupted by breaks for alto saxophone, trombone and banjo, and including a 'talking' muted solo for one of two trumpets, accompanied by the drummer on wood-blocks, with a break by the other trumpet.

Fate Marable at the piano with his band on the SS *Capitol* riverboat in 1920; Armstrong has the cornet, David Jones is the saxophonist, next is the banjoist, Johnny St Cyr, and Baby Dodds is at the drums

The other side is a virtuosic arrangement with the three saxophones tackling 'Pianoflage', a showpiece composed by Roy Bargy, a white ragtime pianist who later became one of the stars of Paul Whiteman's orchestra.

The Whiteman band, at times expanded to an elephantine 30 pieces as if imitating the girth of its 20-stone leader, had set the standard for popular music after the First World War. Because Whiteman crowned himself 'The King of Jazz' while basically performing written dance music with little space for improvisation, jazz-lovers have often ignored the band's strength in playing well-crafted arrangements immaculately. It attracted the social elite of New York to the Palais Royal on Broadway, and it sold an astonishing 1,800,000 copies of its first record, 'Whispering'. The Streckfus brothers were sure that Whiteman's music was the kind of thing their public wanted, and Marable was not going to disappoint them: his men would perform at the same level as Whiteman's. New Orleans musicians began to joke about joining his band as 'going to the conservatory'.

For Armstrong, the sophistication of the parts he had to play came as an unpleasant surprise. But his weakness in reading and theory was quickly noticed by a more experienced band member, David Jones, who took him under his wing and joined the line of Armstrong's mentors behind Peter Davis and Joe Oliver. Although Jones doubled on saxophones for Marable, his main instrument was the mellophone, a hybrid designed to allow trumpeters to produce a sound like a French horn without learning to play one: the mellophone has piston valves instead of rotary, fingered with the right hand instead of the left. Most importantly, Jones was a musician with the gift of teaching, and he gave Armstrong a series of daily tutorials during the intervals in their strenuous working day. *Davey could play that thing so it almost talked to you, and was he hot! He was a trained musician, too, and it was Davey who really taught me to read music. He taught me the value of a note and how to divide and how to phrase and the rest.*[37]

There followed an idyllic period, in which Armstrong developed his skills as an instrumentalist and a reader. He thought of Mark Twain and Tom Sawyer when he recalled it for his first book, *Swing That Music*. Although Armstrong was on board the SS *Sidney'*, he has changed the boat's name: *The 'Dixie Belle' was moving along in almost pitch dark, her paddles making a soft, chunking sound. I could see a few stars high up overhead . . . Above the beat of the paddles, everything was still. The shore seemed a long way off. Could just make it out, going past very slow, like a black wall.*[38] That seems to have more to do with Huckleberry Finn and the runaway slave Jim following the river to freedom than with Tom Sawyer's pranks in the streets of 'St Petersburg', Missouri. But it would be understandable if the writer, whoever he was, decided to avoid the subject of slavery.

Armstrong soon mastered the new repertoire and the technical advances. The pianist Jess Stacy heard him and Baby Dodds in the Marable band when their boat stopped at his home town, Cape Girardeau, Missouri, in 1921: 'I remember one tune they played even now,' he said many years later. 'It was "Whispering", the thing Paul Whiteman had recorded. They just played the hell out of it.'[39] Before long Armstrong was a hero of musicians up and down the river. In St Louis one night he, Jones and Marable were invited to perform on shore by a local bandleader. *We cut loose with one of the very newest hot songs that had just been getting around home when we left – and we let it swing plenty. Every one of us was a natural swing player and didn't need any scoring at all. We almost split that room open.*[40] The leader, who had been vainly trying to get up-to-date New Orleans sounds out of his own musicians, came over and shook their hands. In Davenport, Iowa, 'Bix Beiderbecke and some of the other white musicians came on the boat to listen' and talk to Armstrong, Baby Dodds remembered.[41]

Armstrong also got opportunities to play away from the confinement of the Streckfus-ordained arrangements whenever the boat he was on reached the New Orleans end of a voyage. His growing reputation got him good jobs with leading bands: Henry Allen, the Tuxedo Brass Band, Oscar 'Papa' Celestin and, most importantly, the trombonist Kid Ory, who had shared the leadership of his band with Joe Oliver until Oliver set off for Chicago. Armstrong took Oliver's place when he was available. And while he was lazing around on long trips between towns, *I began to think about Daisy and wish I were with her. I told myself I needed her and she needed me.*[42] At last, in 1921, Armstrong had had enough of the river. Much in demand, he settled back into a routine, and a life with Daisy. Then he got a telegram from Oliver to join his Creole Jazz Band in Chicago.

Cornet Chop Suey

On August 1922, Louis Armstrong played a funeral with the Tuxedo Brass Band and took the 7 pm train to Chicago. He was carrying a trout sandwich his mother had made for him to eat during the journey, but he managed to find a seat next to a woman who had brought a basket full of fried chicken, enough to feed herself and her children for a journey all the way to California, let alone the 900 miles to Chicago: *I lived and ate like a king during the whole trip.*[43] About 11 o'clock the following night, as the train rolled into the Illinois Central station on Michigan Avenue, he was looking anxiously out of the window hoping to see Joe Oliver. A porter recognised him as the young man Oliver had asked him to look out for, and told a taxi-driver to take him to Joe Oliver. Armstrong noticed that his friend and mentor Joe had been crowned King since they last met.

The place he was playing was the Lincoln Gardens Café, a dance hall at 31st Street and Cottage Grove Avenue. It has a special importance for jazz history because it was the place where many young northern musicians, black and white, heard New Orleans music for the first time. The Lincoln Gardens was not a mixed-race 'black-and-tan' venue, but so many white fans wanted to hear the Creole Jazz Band that the management decided to accommodate them on Wednesday nights with a 'Midnight Ramble'. The band stopped playing at 11 pm and the black dancers left. As their own jobs around the town finished, white musicians would trickle in, order drinks, and be waiting when Oliver led his men back on to the stand at midnight. In later years the most important of them would be the cornet player Bix Beiderbecke, from Davenport, and the group of boys from the north-west suburbs

King Oliver (seated) and the Creole Jazz Band: Armstrong is standing fourth from the left

of Chicago who are known as the Austin High School Gang: among them were the great drummer Dave Tough, clarinet-player Frank Teschemacher, tenor saxophonist Bud Freeman, pianist Joe Sullivan and cornet-player Jimmy McPartland.

Left outside the Lincoln Gardens by his taxi, Armstrong was overawed by the city, the building and the sounds of the Creole Jazz Band pounding out into the street. He stood on the pavement, wondering whether to slink off back to New Orleans,

Joe 'King' Oliver (1885–1938) earned his reputation as a cornet-player in the competitive cabarets and brass bands of New Orleans. Along with his strong lead he developed 'freak' techniques, using orthodox mutes and unconventional ones such as bottles, cups and sink-plungers: they enabled him to imitate conversations, animals, a crying baby and other sounds. His blind eye, caused by a boyhood accident or fight, gave him a sinister look, though his kindness was legendary, as was his gargantuan appetite. But pyorrhoea, a gum disease, weakened his teeth and he played less and less. Oliver missed his big chance in New York in 1927: he turned down a job at the Cotton Club because it didn't pay well enough, and young Duke Ellington took his band in there.

until Oliver himself appeared, *and when he saw me, the first words that he said to me were, 'Come on IN HEAH, you little dumb sombitch, we've been waiting for your black ass all night. Ha ha.' Then I was happy and at home just to hear his voice, and enjoyed every moment with him.*[44]

Oliver took Armstrong to his own home for a supper cooked by his wife, Stella, and then to the lodgings he had found for the newcomer. He was astonished to have a private bath: to the sophisticated eyes of Chicagoans there was no doubt he was a country boy. One discerning woman said: 'I wasn't impressed at all, I was very disappointed – 226 pounds. I didn't like anything about him. I didn't like the way he dressed; I didn't like the way he talked; and I just didn't like him. I was very disgusted.'[45] The speaker was Lillian Hardin, a young pianist who was soon to work with Armstrong in Oliver's band. She came from Memphis, Tennessee, but otherwise Oliver had surrounded himself with New Orleans boys: clarinet-player Johnny Dodds and his drummer brother Warren, nicknamed Baby, trombonist Honoré Dutrey, and a series of banjoists or bass-players from the same city.

What they were providing, for the 700 or so people who squeezed into the Lincoln Gardens every night to dance the bunny-hug or the foxtrot, was stomping music in the now well-established New Orleans style: a group of musicians playing as one, with solo contributions largely confined to 'breaks' – out-of-tempo unaccompanied interruptions at the end of a phrase in the tune. The rest of the time the band improvised together, following a lead by the cornet-player, who normally stayed close to the melody. The trombone chose notes in the bass or the tenor register, often using glissandos in what was called the tailgate style, from the wagons which often carried New Orleans bands; and the clarinet was free to create an obbligato out of a bubbling line of quavers. Meanwhile the rhythm section laid down a steady, pulsating 4/4.

There was no need for a second cornet, which would have to play an inner part and so increase the risk of the front-line players getting in each other's way. So why was Oliver so keen for Armstrong to join him? One possible explanation is that he was no longer confident in his own powers: his teeth were beginning to give him trouble. Another is that he had spotted Armstrong as a potential competitor, and wanted him on his side rather than working for any rival leader. A third is simply that he recognised his unique talents, and thought they would add to the appeal of the band. They soon discovered that they could work together to make duet breaks and astonish the public. The trombonist Preston Jackson saw them often at the Lincoln Gardens: 'Oh boy! Did those two team together? When you saw Joe lean over towards Louis at the first ending you would know they were going to make a break in the middle of the next chorus. And what breaks they made. Louis never knew what Joe was going to play, but he would always follow him perfectly. Louis was, and is, as good a second trumpet as he is a first; he never missed.'[46]

The first recordings of jazz were made in 1917 in New York by a group of white New Orleans players, led by the cornet-player Nick La Rocca, who called themselves the Original Dixieland Jazz (or Jass) Band and were resident at Reisenweber's Restaurant near Columbus Circle. They recorded two sides in January for Columbia, which lost its nerve and failed to issue them. Victor recorded the band instead, and cashed in. 'Livery Stable Blues' is a 'novelty' number, with cornet and trombone playing the parts of a horse and a cow; with 'Dixie Jass Band One-Step' it triggered the Jazz Age of flappers, Stutz Bearcats, raccoon coats and hip-flasks, which was to dominate America's white middle-class youth until 1929. By 1919 the ODJB had exported themselves and the jazz craze to London, and other white groups were recording. The first black jazz band to record had to wait until 1921, when Kid Ory took 'Spikes' Seven Pods of Pepper' into a

Los Angeles studio for two sides, with Mutt Carey playing elegant lead cornet. But although the ODJB records have many admirers they sound frantic to others – apparently they had to play fast to get their numbers into three minutes – and the classic period of jazz recording starts in the Starr Piano Company's makeshift studio at Richmond, Indiana, 200 miles from Chicago, on 5 April 1923, the year in which the runaway song was certainly not a jazz hit: 'Yes! We Have No Bananas'.

Starr had begun to make gramophones under the name Gennett, and needed records for customers to play on them, so, before the invention of microphones, the Creole Jazz Band gathered around an acoustic horn to make their first recordings. A musician who recorded for Gennett in 1922 described 'the barn-like studios and the primitive recording mechanism – a turntable mounted on a frame of 3/4" pipes – a massive turntable with a three-ball governor to regulate the speed, and a series of weights that had to be cranked up like a grandfather hall clock.'[47] As you might expect, the Oliver Gennetts are not easy on the modern ear, though recent transfers have revealed many of their hidden beauties. So you can hear Louis's distinctive open tone on 'Chimes Blues' when he has his first recorded solo: it sounds as if he has been practising it, until he takes a rhythmic liberty in his last couple of bars. The next day Oliver demonstrated his own style in a muted solo on 'Dippermouth Blues', which became permanently attached to the tune; in June he played it again for an OKeh recording with better sound and a powerful Armstrong lead, and less than two years later Louis would record it as a member of Fletcher Henderson's Orchestra – each time, of course, with someone yelling out 'Oh, play that thing!' The second day's session also produced an example of the famous duet breaks, on 'Snake Rag'. On 'Tears', recorded in October, Louis gets a chance to show his developing virtuosity in a brilliant series of solo breaks.

The 37 sides that survive of the Creole Jazz Band's recordings, all in 1923, are full of joyful, forthright exuberance. They are the pinnacle of the New Orleans ensemble style as seen through Oliver's disciplined vision. But at the end of the recordings, the days of the Creole Jazz Band were numbered. It set off on a tour of the Middle West, but with different personnel. Lil Hardin said that Johnny Dodds found out that Oliver had been collecting $95 a week in wages for each band member, but paying them only $75. He and his brother Baby threatened to beat Oliver up, and Oliver started bringing a pistol to work; the Dodds brothers quit the band, along with Dutrey. 'Louis was always crazy about Joe, you know he was his idol, so he wouldn't quit. If Louis wouldn't quit, so naturally I wouldn't quit.'[48]

Naturally, because while Lil had been helping Armstrong with his sight-reading and choosing his new wardrobe, they had also been dating. And when their divorces were finalised, Armstrong's from Daisy and Lil from her husband, a singer named Jimmy Johnson they were married, on 5 February 1924: Lil wore 'a Parisian gown of white crêpe elaborately beaded in rhinestones and silver beads'.[49] She promptly bought an eleven-room house on East 44th Street, and moved her mother in with them. Armstrong sent for Clarence, now eight years old. The people who had been looking after him tied a label to his coat, put him on a train, and he moved in as well. Mayann was also living nearby, having come up to Chicago to keep an eye on her son, but she went back to New Orleans once she saw him settled. Armstrong invited her for a farewell night out around the nightspots: *How about you and me going out and having a real grand time just by ourselves, no one else. She agreed right away, and the police had to show both of us where we lived the next morning.*[50] In 1927 Mayann returned to Chicago, suffering from hardening of the arteries: Armstrong paid for her hospital care at $17 a day, but could not save her. *I never forget what Mother told me before she died. She said: "Son – carry on, you're a good boy treats everybody right, and everybody, white and coloured, loves you. You have a good heart, you can't miss."*[51]

The ambitious Lil is usually held responsible for splitting Armstrong away from Oliver to advance his career by going to New York, but some time later Oliver told the cornet-player Rex Stewart that he had stayed in Chicago 'for two good reasons, both of them spelled "syndicate". No booking agent wanted to incur the ill will of the Chicago syndicate that operated the club (Lincoln Gardens) where they played. Even if an agent dared attempt a New York deal, there was no place in New York where they could play.'[52]

At last, in June, Louis quit the King and went into a band at the Dreamland nightclub, led by a singing drummer, Ollie Powers. Then he got an invitation from the bandleader Fletcher Henderson, who had first heard him and offered him a job while passing through New Orleans in 1922. On 29 September 1924, after explaining to King Oliver that this would be his one big chance, Louis Armstrong took the train to New York City.

The dancers who came to the Roseland Dance Palace on Broadway at West 51st Street in midtown Manhattan were white. They foxtrotted to Fletcher Henderson's band with the same kind of enthusiasm as their parents had done the dance when it was new, just invented by the white stars of the ballrooms, Vernon and Irene Castle, accompanied by James Reese Europe's orchestra of black virtuosi.

Europe's men were skilled instrumentalists and fluent sight-readers. But their white audiences liked to think of them as simple folk-artists who had no formal musical education, so they learned their parts in rehearsal and appeared in public with big grins and no sheet-music. Henderson's men did not resort to this subterfuge, but they did rehearse assiduously, and Henderson himself described Louis's first rehearsal: 'We had a medley of Irish waltzes in the book, an intricate, well-marked arrangement. One passage began triple fortissimo, and then it suddenly softened down on the next passage to double pianissimo. The score was properly marked "pp" to indicate the pianissimo, but when everybody else softened down, there was Louis, still blowing as hard as he could. I stopped the band, and told him – pretty sharply, I guess – that in this band we read the marks as well as the notes. I asked him if he could read the marks, and he said he could. But then I asked him: "What about 'pp'?" and he answered: *"Why, it means pound plenty."*[53]

Henderson preferred another trumpeter, Joe Smith, a beautifully lyrical soloist who had been in and out of the band several times. But Smith joined the revue 'Chocolate Dandies', and Henderson had to agree to the demands of his musical director, the brilliant reed-player and arranger Don Redman, and hire Louis instead. He had a revolutionary impact on the band, on Redman's arranging style, and – through the wide exposure he got through Henderson's performances and records – on the expanding jazz community of musicians and fans. Henderson insisted that working in a band that played in such unusual keys, for the time, as E and D 'put the finishing touches to his playing . . . But he influenced the band greatly, too, by making the men really swing-conscious with that New Orleans style of his.'[54] Redman would set the style for the big bands of the swing era by writing call-and-response passages which pitted the brass section against the reeds: he also used the simple repeated figures called riffs, and Henderson himself turned to writing exciting, swinging arrangements, many of

Fletcher Henderson (1897–1952). Born into a middle-class black family in Georgia, Henderson graduated from Atlanta University in chemistry and mathematics, and came to New York to find post-graduate work. Instead he became a song-plugger for black publishers, and it was finding accompaniments for their records which turned him into a pianist and bandleader. In 1939 Henderson broke up his band and went to work for Benny Goodman as an arranger. A comeback attempt ended when he had a stroke in 1950: he never played again.

which he sold to Benny Goodman when he had a cash crisis in 1934, providing the Goodman band with the foundation of its success and sparking off the swing era.

Henderson's band opened the Roseland residency at one end of the dance floor; Sam Lanin's white band occupied the bandstand at the opposite end, and they soon spread the word among musicians about the new trumpet soloist. A couple of weeks after the opening Armstrong was in the Columbia studio, taking his first solo with Henderson on 'Go 'Long Mule', a novelty number dominated by doo-wacka-doo section-work and farmyard imitations, in which even Armstrong joins: but his flowing solo later shows a rhythmic freedom unknown to the men playing with him. Overwhelmingly, the Henderson records show this contrast between Armstrong's relaxed way with the beat and the well-schooled rigidity of the band. On 'Everybody Loves My Baby' Louis plays the theme as a solo over the rhythm section, the reeds taking the middle eight, before the performance bogs down in over-careful ensemble work and an overlong banjo solo: then the famous voice, already gravelly at 23, is heard on record for the first time as Armstrong interrupts the coda with some shouts of encouragement:

Ow brother, don't play me that!
Ah, now you come to do it!
Oh, that's it, boy![55]

Fletcher never allowed him to sing again on records or on stage, and Armstrong resented it. *He had a million-dollar talent in his band and he never thought enough to let me sing or nothing,*[56] he told an interviewer in 1960.

When Henderson had first heard Armstrong in New Orleans he had recognised his potential as a blues accompanist, and he hurried him into the studios to begin a remarkable series of records with the women who were riding on top of the 'blues craze' that had started in 1920 with Mamie Smith's million-selling record of (appropriately) 'Crazy Blues'. In just over a year Louis took part in recordings with a dozen or so singers, the most famous of whom was the great Bessie Smith.

Bessie Smith (1894–1937). A leading performer in black touring shows, Bessie Smith was brought into the recording studios by Clarence Williams in 1923. Her first issued record, 'Down-hearted Blues', helped to build her into the greatest of the vaudeville singers who ruled the black theatre circuits in the 20s. Her powerful, expressive voice and majestic stage manner earned her the title 'Empress of the Blues'. But the Depression and her own drinking wrecked her career. She recorded one last session in 1933 for white fans in Europe and carried on touring until her death after a car crash in Mississippi.

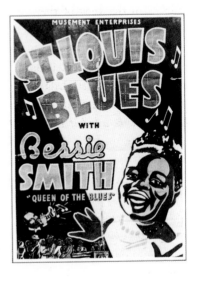

Their first record together was 'St Louis Blues', and it seems as though Armstrong got off on the wrong foot. His obbligato is an equal voice with Bessie's, foreshadowing some of her phrases rather than commenting on what she has sung, as if he were impatient with the Empress's stately tempo. The next record, in the same session, is 'Reckless Blues': Armstrong uses a wa-wa mute like King Oliver, and it stifles his forthright style into dec-oration. He is similarly reticent in his other records with Bessie. She preferred Joe Smith, so perhaps Fred Longshaw, her musical director, reined in Armstrong's enthusiasm. *No rehearsal,* he remembered, *I was there to make the records, didn't get to talking to her too much, don't think we spoke the same kind of language.*[57]

Recording sessions helped Armstrong make ends meet – Henderson was paying him $55 a week, $20 less than King Oliver – and he soon found himself in the studio under the leadership of an old acquaintance from New Orleans: Clarence Williams, pianist, publisher, record-producer, talent-scout . . . and 'a real horse-thief',[58] in the view of the bassist Pops Foster. While Williams was still a teenager he and Armond J Piron had set up a music business based on Williams's ability to transcribe music on to paper as fast as it was played. Louis saw him doing it while he was on the bandstand at Pete Lala's with Kid Ory, performing a song he had thought of himself, about a prostitute named Katie. *When I had finished he asked if I would sell the number to him. He mentioned $25,* Armstrong told the publicist Ernie Anderson. *So I said, 'Okay,' and he handed me some forms to sign and I signed them. He said he'd be back with the cash. But he never did come back.*[59] The partners cleaned up the lyrics, put Piron's name on the song, and had an international hit with 'I Wish I Could Shimmy Like My Sister Kate'. When the partnership with Piron collapsed, Williams moved to Chicago and then to New York, bringing his business methods with him, but also providing work for musicians in a long line of records aimed at the growing African-American market in the northern cities. Williams's music is by turns earthy and nostalgic, and much

Sidney Bechet (1897–1959), already a formidable clarinet player, was praised by the eminent Swiss conductor Ernest Ansermet after performing in London in 1919. Bechet took up the straight soprano saxophone on the same visit. The soprano's greater power and the wide vibrato he used on it allowed him to dominate – some would say bully – the bands he played with, mainly in Europe during the 20s. Back in America he led classic recordings by the New Orleans Feetwarmers in 1932, a hit record of 'Summertime' in 1939, and the Big Four sessions with Muggsy Spanier in 1940. Bechet settled in France after the war, becoming a national hero and scoring another hit with 'Petite Fleur' in 1952. His autobiography was published after his death in Paris.

of it has great beauty. He worked entirely in the studio, usually with singers and small bands, starting with the legendary Blue Five: cornet, clarinet, trombone, piano and banjo. The personnel he assembled depended on who was available in New York at the time, and in late 1924 two who were available were Armstrong and Sidney Bechet.

They were evenly matched in virtuosity and imagination, and Bechet was gradually moving away from the limpid or acidic tones the clarinet brought to the New Orleans ensemble. He preferred the soprano saxophone, a broad-toned, muscular instrument which in his hands snarled and growled like a young tiger. It made him as loud as Armstrong, and their Blue Five records are excitingly balanced between the cooperation required by the contrapuntal New Orleans form and the competition created by two powerful players slugging it out like prizefighters. The peak of the series is probably 'Cake-Walking Babies from Home', made in January 1925, with a vocal by Williams's wife, Eva Taylor, a singer capable of tackling anything from parlour ballads to raunchy blues in a rich contralto with a well-controlled vibrato rather like the one Armstrong was developing on the cornet. She strides into the lyrics of 'Cake-Walking', breaks into a sort of exalted declamation near the end, and sets her ordinarily rather staid husband pounding the keyboard to send Armstrong off on a stomping final chorus. The other recording the Blue Five made that day is quite different, a racial protest song about a bullied child, disguised as a sentimental southern melody. But 'Pickin' on Your Baby', too, demonstrates Armstrong's growing skill, this time as a high-note player. After Eva's vocal, Louis stays in her key for a solo that keeps close to the melody. As the Williams expert Tom Lord pointed out: 'In the key of C (D on his horn) it keeps him up around A and B above the stave, quite a bit, having him end on a high D – all with perfect control.'[60] On the other hand on some sides, such as 'Court House Blues' with

Clara Smith, he uses the absence of a trombone as an opportunity to play in the bottom of his instrument's range.

Armstrong and Bechet had recorded another 'Cake-Walking' a fortnight earlier, calling themselves the Red Onion Jazz Babies and backing the singers Alberta Hunter and Clarence Todd. There was only one difference in the band: the piano player was Lil Hardin, visiting Armstrong during a break from her job in Chicago. A slightly slacker tempo, a quavery vocal duet and Hardin's Palm Court style make it a less intense performance than the Blue Five's: Armstrong takes the opportunity in his solo to rhapsodise rather than drive for the finish. There had been a hope that Armstrong and Hardin would be back together after the Henderson band's long residency at Roseland ended at the end of May 1925, but a booking for the band in Chicago fell through, and Henderson led his men out on a tour of New England based at Lawrence, Massachusetts. *We were the first coloured big band to hit the road*, Armstrong remembered. There were days off when he and the clarinet player Buster Bailey could go swimming in the Merrimac River.

Of course I am not so bad myself at swimming. In fact it's one of my favourite hobbies, outside of typing – I loves that also.[61]

When summer ended, Armstrong returned to New York, already a hero to musicians. Rex Stewart, then an 18-year-old cornet-player, wrote later: 'Louis was a musician's musician. I was only one of his ardent admirers. I tried to walk like him, talk like him. I bought shoes and a suit like the Great One wore.'[62] But when Lil next visited New York she saw how Henderson was treating her husband, and found that he was still not putting Armstrong where a star should be: on the playbills. She went back to Chicago, fixed him up with a job in her band at the Dreamland Café at $75 a week, and told him to give in his notice. Armstrong talked Henderson into handing his chair over to Rex

Stewart, Henderson gave Armstrong a generous farewell party, and Louis was sick over Henderson's tuxedo.

Armstrong came back to Chicago at the beginning of November, to a promise from Lil Hardin – which he did not believe – that he would be earning $75 a week, and a banner across the place where they were playing which said: 'Louis Armstrong: the World's Greatest Cornet Player'. A week later, in the OKeh Record Company's studio, he would begin to prove it in his first session as a leader. Over the next three years Armstrong and a handful of musicians would build the most important monument of recorded jazz, a concentrated series of performances that has never been equalled. The labels on the first sides said they were by Louis Armstrong's Hot Five, and later sessions were by his Hot Seven, his Savoy Ballroom Five, and his Orchestra. The numbers of musicians might be as many as ten or as few as two.

They are not perfect, or even consistent, and some are forgettable. But they include masterpieces that encapsulate the spirit of

The Hot Five: Armstrong, Johnny St Cyr, Johnny Dodds, Kid Ory and Lil Hardin

jazz in the three-minute boundaries of the ten-inch 78rpm record. They also show the direction jazz was to take, which would emphasise the improvising soloist supported or challenged by the ensemble. Their starting point, however, was New Orleans: all but one of the original Hot Five came from there, and all but one – a different one – had played together in King Oliver's band. Basically, they played in the New Orleans style of 'collective improvisation', but the lighter texture of the ensemble, and the superior quality of OKeh's recording, allowed the different wind instruments to be heard clearly as individuals rather than contributors to a group sound. From the Oliver band came Lil Hardin, Johnny Dodds and the banjoist Johnny St Cyr. Armstrong's old leader from New Orleans, Kid Ory, joined on trombone: he said he had come to Chicago from California at the request of Armstrong, and that at first the whole Hot Five were members of Lil's Dreamland band. The Hot Five appeared only twice as such in public, alongside other well-known bands in concerts arranged by the black branch of the musicians' union, Local No. 208.

'Our recording sessions would start this way,' Ory said. 'The OKeh people would call up Louis and say they wanted so many sides. They never told him what numbers they wanted or how they wanted them . . . After we'd make a side, Louis would say, "Was that all right?" And if one of us thought we could do it over and do it better, why Louis would tell them to do it again, and so we would do it over.'[63]

Johnny Dodds (1892–1940), a self-taught player from Uptown, left New Orleans to join King Oliver with his clarinet wrapped in newspaper. His expressive and beautiful blues-playing, particularly in the lower register, earned him the admiring nickname 'Toilet' and made him a favourite of the South Side audience and one of the musicians most imitated by the young fans who joined the revival of traditional jazz in the 1930s and 1940s. During the Depression Dodds drove a cab in Chicago, but the revival of interest in New Orleans music brought him work and recording dates before he died of a stroke.

The Hot Five recordings may have begun at the initiative of Richard Myknee Jones, a pianist and composer who was a Chicago equivalent to Clarence Williams, and the inspiration may have been the two studio bands Louis had played with in New York, the Blue Five and the Red Onion Jazz Babies. There were plenty of 'Fives' around, working in cafés and dance halls, and it was probably as high a number as the recording engineers could cope with. At the first session, on Thursday, 12 November 1925, starting at 9 or 10 o'clock in the morning, the Hot Five produced three tunes for issue: there is no way of knowing how many tries it took them, because OKeh routinely destroyed spoiled masters and kept no written log of them. The first successful side was 'My Heart', a tightly played pop song, but the session got more intense with 'Yes! I'm in the Barrel' and finished with 'Gut Bucket Blues', a cheerful series of solos linked by Louis's shouted encouragement and ending with his own powerful contribution, starting in the lower part of the cornet's range and driving a final ensemble.

Two sessions later, on Friday, 26 February 1926, both Hardin and Armstrong sang about the 'Georgia Grind', a dance everybody's trying to do. Next, over Johnny St Cyr's banjo, Armstrong sang some of the words to 'Heebie Jeebies' – which, not surprisingly, turns out to be a dance – and this is one version of what he sang next:

> *Eeff, gaff, mmmff, dee-bo, duh deedle-la bahm,*
> *Rip-bip-ee-doo-dee-doot, doo,*
> *Roo-dee-doot duh-dee-dut-duh-dut,*
> *Dee-dut-dee-dut-doo, dee-doo-dee-doo-dee-doo-dut,*
> *Skeep, skam, skip-bo-dee-dah-dee-dat, doop-dum-dee,*
> *Frantic rhythm, so come on down, do that dance,*
> *They call the heebie jeebies dance, sweet mammo,*
> *Poppa's got to do the heebie jeebies dance.*[64]

And then the rest of the band returned to end the performance. Armstrong claimed afterwards that he had accidentally dropped the sheet-music and made up sounds to fit the tune until he could pick it up again. But it is at least as likely that he planned to depart from his text: his initial trumpet chorus on the record is subdued, as if he is keeping something up his sleeve.

When I finished the record I just knew the recording people would throw it out, Louis wrote in a retrospect of some of his early records in 1951. *And to my surprise they all came running out of the controlling booth and said – 'Leave that in.'*[65] The outcome was sensational: sales of OKeh 8300 reached 40,000 within weeks, in an era when 10,000 sales made a success. Although scat singing was not new to records – Don Redman recorded 'My Papa Doesn't Two-time No Time' with Henderson in April 1924 – and Armstrong himself said later that he was only doing what he had done with his boyhood barber-shop quartet in the streets of New Orleans, the public loved the novelty and his distinctive sawmill voice. Armstrong sings on a lot of these records, and his warm, intimate delivery saves some sets of lyrics that would have been better dropped on the floor, such as 'Irish Black Bottom'.

'Muskrat Ramble' was on the other side of 'Heebie Jeebies', and won a permanent place in the jazz repertoire: the band went on over the next months to make instrumental showpieces such as 'Cornet Chop Suey' and 'Struttin' with Some Barbecue', tunes Armstrong wrote, he claimed, because of his love of food. The clarinet of Johnny Dodds shines in many of these sides with a stark beauty of phrasing, and he and Ory maintain some of the New Orleans atmosphere, even though they are gradually being pushed into the background. This band is not a cooperative effort. Dodds sounds less inhibited when the Hot Five turned up in the Vocalion studio, masquerading as 'Lil's Hot Shots', to record 'Georgia Bo Bo' and

'Drop That Sack' *(some cat's stealing chickens*[66] was Armstrong's explanation of the title). The legend is that Richard Myknee Jones played the record for Armstrong and warned him about breaking his OKeh contract: he assured him that he wasn't the trumpet-player on the record, and that he wouldn't do it again. Since there is a characteristic Armstrong vocal on 'Georgia Bo Bo', and Jones was also working for Vocalion, the story may not be true.

Armstrong went to Vocalion again, as a sideman in Johnny Dodds's Black Bottom Stompers, a seven-piece band, and within a fortnight led his first Hot Seven session, with Johnny's brother Baby on drums: the introduction of electrical recording meant that he was no longer restricted to wood-blocks, as he had been with King Oliver, but could use his cymbals. In one week in May 1927 the Hot Seven recorded eleven titles. In a stop-time solo on 'Potato Head Blues' (which is not really blues) Armstrong demonstrates an eloquence of tone and phrasing that, for sheer command and poise, is reminiscent of Caruso, a singer Louis much admired. But he himself wrote that he was remembering King Oliver playing in New Orleans at the Pelican Dance Hall: *Every note that I blew in this recording, I thought of Papa Joe.*[67] Louis introduces '12th Street Rag', a number that was corny as soon as it was written by one Euday L Bowman in 1919, by wittily shifting the balance of his phrases so that the repetitive rhythm of the tune is tamed.

Armstrong found new inspiration when he added the guitarist Lonnie Johnson for two Hot Five sessions: he brings a new, swinging rhythm to 'Hotter than That' and 'Savoy Blues'. When the Hot Five re-convened six months later in June 1928, Armstrong was the only remaining member of the original group. On drums was his Streckfus Line shipmate, Zutty Singleton. From the Carroll Dickerson band, which Armstrong was then fronting, came the smooth trombonist Fred Robinson, the harsh-toned clarinet-player Jimmy Strong, the banjoist Mancy Cara and Louis's new musical partner, the pianist Earl Hines. This is no longer the comfortable world where the Hot Five began, a few friends earning a little extra money. The musician-critic Richard Hadlock wrote of 'Don't Jive Me': 'The trumpeter and pianist constantly challenge themselves by starting phrases that cannot possibly fit the arrangement, then squirming out of them just in time to save the performance. It was breathtakingly daring music that set a terrifying pace for young jazzmen.'[68] Fusing this new experimental spirit with his earlier lyricism, Armstrong arrived at 'West End Blues', thought by many to be the greatest of all his recordings. It starts with a cascade of notes, an arresting out-of-tempo cadenza that settles into an heroic statement of the powerful blues theme. Then comes a passage in which Louis exchanges wordless vocal phrases with the clarinet. He raises the tension with a single note held for nearly four bars before launching into a series of repeated falling phrases echoing the opening cadenza. Between the various parts of Armstrong's performance Robinson and Hines take solos, but for the listener they are resting-places before Louis's titanic emotional force returns. 'West End Blues' – the title comes from the resort on Lake Pontchartrain, at the end of a tram line from New Orleans – is a deeply moving blues performance and at the same time a perfectly shaped miniature concerto, an improvised work of art.

In Hines, Armstrong had met a musical match: while he brought his rhythmic daring to the partnership, Hines brought harmonic invention. So when the Chicago recordings of small groups ended, three years after they began, they were on a higher musical plane partly because of the new pianist. Armstrong is traditionally credited with having influenced Hines into inventing 'trumpet-style' piano. Hines's right hand played a melody, often in octaves to make it heard over the

Earl Hines (1903–83) left Pittsburgh, his home town, at the age of 20 to play piano in Chicago, making historic records with the clarinet-player Jimmie Noone as well as Armstrong. At 25 he started his own band at the Grand Terrace café, where a radio announcer gave him the nickname 'Fatha'. The Hines band became a laboratory for bebop pioneers including Charlie Parker and Dizzy Gillespie before it broke up in 1947. After three years with Armstrong's All Stars, Hines worked mainly in the San Francisco area with Dixieland groups until 1964, when three New York appearances revived a career that continued until his death.

rest of the band, using short phrases imitating a solo wind instrument and tremolo in place of vibrato. His left hand accompanied independently, with a great deal of rhythmic freedom that no longer relied on ragtime. Hines claimed that his style was formed before he worked with Armstrong, and it may be that he had as much influence on Louis as Louis had on him.

Hines's first instrument had been the trumpet, but he had the advanced harmonic knowledge gained from classical piano studies. Players of instruments which are capable of playing chords are naturally exposed to harmony at a formative stage, and they can make suprising choices of notes when they can also play a single-line instrument: an outstanding example is Bobby Hackett, the cornet-player and guitarist who was one of Louis's favourites. For Armstrong and Hines, the seal on the partnership was set by their recording of 'Weather Bird', a duet version of a number Armstrong had played with King Oliver. In the hands of the two young jazz lions, it is so fleet and the ideas twist and turn so quickly that it seems like an inspiration snatched out of thin air.

Muggles

Outside the studio, Armstrong was the toast of the South Side. He had felt dissatisfied as soon as he started playing for Lil at Dreamland, a 'black and tan' dance hall with its entrance right on South State Street, the centre of black entertainment. Lil, he wrote later, *had a nice little Swing Band – but not like Fletcher's*.[69] Still, after a month there Armstrong became so popular that he got an offer from Erskine Tate, who was leading a 20-piece band at the Vendome Theater, a cinema four blocks north on State Street. As was usual in the bigger cinemas in the silent era, Tate's band played accompaniments to the picture, and in the intermission entertained the audience with *Overtures etc. and then they'd finish up with a Red Hot Number*.[70]

This is what used to happen: 'Louis, all smiles, climbed out of the pit, toting his cornet in one hand and his indispensable handkerchief in the other. Instantly the house was in an uproar, feet stamping on the floor, cheers and whistles rending the air. A few preliminary flourishes of the handkerchief and Louis was off on his feature number, "Heebie Jeebies". Before he hit the second note they were swaying back and forth in their seats all the way to the last row. He kept that up for a while and as suddenly picked up a little megaphone and in a husky voice poured forth the words of the song with all the warmth of the Southland. He took another vocal chorus, not with words but with a guttural mouthing of incoherent nonsense, supplemented with unearthly grimaces.'[71]

Lil had threatened to skin him alive if he turned down the job with Tate, and he quickly saw the benefits of working in a movie theatre: *I became quite a figure at the Vendome. Especially with*

Lil Hardin (1898–1971). Although she exaggerated her qualifications – she had not graduated in music from Fisk University, Nashville, as she later claimed, but had dropped out after a year – she probably did know more theory than other members of the Creole Jazz Band or the Hot Five, and could write down their compositions for publication. *Read music, yes – as an improviser – hmmm – terrible,*[74] was Armstrong's judgement. After they separated, Lil continued to call herself Armstrong and work as a pianist, singer and bandleader, making some interesting records for Decca in the 1930s. While playing in Chicago at a memorial concert a few weeks after Armstrong's death, Lil collapsed with a heart attack and died.

the gals. I met Alpha during the time I was working there. Alpha was a cute young girl 19 years old when she used to come to the Vendome Theatre twice a week[72] when the programme changed, always sitting in the front row. *She would sit right where I could get a good look at her. And she had big pretty eyes anyway – I couldn't keep from digging her. There were times when Lil would be in the Vendome at the same time as Alpha. Well – on those nights we couldn't flirt so much.*[73]

Justifying his infidelities with the line that Lil *had been running around with one of the Chicago pimps while I was at work* [75] and that they were always having rows at home, Armstrong pursued his affair with Alpha Smith, visiting the white family where she worked as a nursemaid and taking Clarence to see her mother, Florence Smith, and her husband, Mr Woods, in their *very dingy apartment with a wooden bath tub*[76] in a poor district near the Lincoln Gardens. Clarence said that he found the Smiths' home more relaxing and that he would rather live with them. It was the excuse Armstrong was looking for, after another row with Lil: *I immediately moved Clarence's bags and baggage – all his clothes and mine and we both moved down at 33rd and Cottage Grove Ave. with Mrs Smith, Mr Woods and Alpha. Hooray.*[77]

By that time Armstrong joined Carroll Dickerson's big band at the Sunset Café, starting work there after 11 o'clock, when he finished the last of four shows at the Vendome. He was making plenty of money, and spending it on Alpha: $90 overcoats and

Sunday drives out of the city in his new Ford with the yellow wire wheels. The Sunset band also had Earl Hines on piano, and another partnership just as significant for Armstrong started there: its boss was a small-timer with mob connections and an obsession with young girls. His name was Joe Glaser.

In his first significant act, Glaser fired Dickerson, who was drinking too much to play his violin, and Armstrong found himself fronting a band named the Stompers, playing for shows with twelve dancers, twelve showgirls, comedians, singers and speciality acts. He had his name in lights in Chicago, then the capital city of jazz, and the white faces in the audience included members of the Whiteman band when it was in town: Bix Beiderbecke, maybe, or Bing Crosby, as well as local kids like Benny Goodman, carrying his clarinet in a sack, or Tommy Dorsey, still not certain whether to concentrate on cornet or trombone. There was also a slightly older clarinet-player called Milton Mezzrow, or Mezz, which was also the name for the high-grade Mexican marijuana that was his main way of making a living, because he didn't have the talent to earn one as a musician. Louis became a fan, and paid tribute by recording a blues named 'Muggles', one of the many names for marijuana which, presumably, the OKeh company had not heard.

In 1927 Armstrong's singing took a new turn: instead of the guttural tone for which he was already famous, he began to use a light, crooning 'head voice' for pop songs such as 'I Can't Give You Anything But Love'. He dropped it in 1930, and it may be that his vocal cords had lost their flexibility. Linda Hirst, the Head of Vocal Studies at Trinity College of Music, London, said: 'Purist singing teachers would say that no one can go on singing the way he sang because you wouldn't have any vocal cords left – but the vocal cords are a lot stronger than people think. I would say because he used a microphone he wasn't doing himself much further harm.'[78]

The Depression was already biting in Chicago, and African-Americans were among the first to have no disposable income for nights out on the town. Armstrong's steady companions were Hines and the drummer, Zutty Singleton – always pronounced Zooty. So when the Sunset closed its doors, and a restaurant job in the Loop downtown didn't work out, they were all broke together. They rented a little place on the West Side to run their own dance, but at intermission a drunk came in holding a .45 and pointed it at the bandstand. *Earl Hines tried to go through his upright piano, and heaven knows where Zutty and I went, but I know we came off that bandstand right away. Somebody went and found the cops from somewhere out that way, and they chased that black sommitch downstairs, and this drunken guy ran under a house, and the cops shot all up under that house and filled that guy full of holes.*[79] The drunk turned out to have shot a policeman the week before; the audience never came back. 'We had some gigs then that paid only three or four dollars a night,' Hines remembered. 'Louis's wife was booking us at the time, and we played some dances where the average good-thinking person wouldn't even dream of going. But we couldn't be choicy, and we had to play wherever she booked us. Sometimes we got our money and sometimes we didn't.'[80] In the end Hines went to work with Jimmie Noone at the Apex Club and Carroll Dickerson hired Louis and Zutty for a job at the Savoy Ballroom, newly opened in Chicago.

But eventually business dried up there, as well, so when Tommy Rockwell of OKeh sent a telegram asking Armstrong to return to New York to work, he showed it to the band and they agreed to go as a package, driving across country. They arrived, broke of course, to find that Rockwell had no booking for the band: he had wanted Armstrong by himself, to go into a musical called 'Great Day'. Armstrong demanded, and eventually got, money to feed, house and re-clothe the band and within a fortnight Rockwell had booked them in to Connie's Inn, a club at 131st Street and 7th Avenue, near the centre of Harlem. In the meanwhile Louis had gone to Philadelphia to join the 'Great Day' company, and been fired by Vincent Youmans, the composer and producer: the show lasted only 36 performances when it reached New York. Armstrong was back there before it, working at a theatre in the evenings and then hurrying to lead his band in a nightclub. The show he was in was 'Hot Chocolates', which ran for 219 performances on Broadway.

It had a score by Fats Waller

Some time in 1928 Armstrong switched permanently from playing cornet to trumpet, having tried both instruments on and off for a year or so. Cornet tone is mellow, trumpet tone more brilliant. The bore of a cornet is conical rather than cylindrical, as is a trumpet's, but the difference became less exaggerated in later models, and Bill Berry, who played cornet in the Duke Ellington band, said that the only difference in modern instruments is that the cornet's valves are easier to reach for players with short arms.[81]

and Harry Brooks and lyrics by Andy Razaf: Armstrong's big number was 'Ain't Misbehavin''. With the band from Connie's Inn, he recorded it and three other songs from the show, including 'Black and Blue'. Over lightly scored saxophones he sings a lament originally about a dark-skinned woman who has lost her lighter-skinned lover: but, as the critic Dan Morgenstern pointed out, by leaving out the relevant verse Armstrong turns the chorus into a universal complaint against racism, singing *My only sin is in my skin.* Earlier he had taken part in the first inter-racial jazz recording, with three black musicians and three white, one of them the trombonist Jack Teagarden. Because the date was for 8 am they stayed up all night with a gallon jug of whiskey. They recorded two numbers, one of them an instrumental blues, and the engineer asked its name. Louis 'saw the empty jug sitting in the middle of the floor and said, *Man, we sure knocked that jug – you can call it "Knockin' a Jug".* And that's the name that went on the record.'[82]

The Luis Russell band in 1930; the musicians are (left to right) Henry 'Red' Allen, Greely Walton, Paul Barbarin, Charlie Holmes, Russell, Albert Nicholas, Will Johnson, Pops Foster, J C Higginbotham and Otis Johnson

The same day, with a band that was basically the Luis Russell orchestra, dominated by New Orleans musicians, he made two contrasting records. 'Mahogany Hall Stomp', named after Lulu White's Storyville brothel, is launched at a loping trot by Pops Foster bowing a string bass, not the conventional tuba of the time, and he soon switches to pizzicato – the flowing rhythm reminded the composer-critic Gunther Schuller of the recordings made two years earlier in New Orleans by the wonderful Sam Morgan band. Armstrong takes a muted solo which summarises the elements he would use for the rest of his career in building improvisations: repeated rhythmical phrases; a long-held single note (under Lonnie Johnson's guitar solo); and repetitions of a single note. The excitement Armstrong builds does not flag in the parts where he is silent, because the other soloists – Johnson, the alto-player Charlie Holmes and the trombonist J C Higginbotham – have learned his lessons about rhythmic flexibility.

Three saxophones provide the harmonies underneath, as they do on the other side of the original 78, 'I Can't Give You Anything But Love': its slower tempo reveals a whine and a wobble, the result of a none-too-successful attempt to imitate the band Louis loved, Guy Lombardo and his Royal Canadians. Their billing called it 'The Sweetest Music this Side of Heaven', but one review noted 'the exaggerated sax vibratos, the clippety brass phrases with their illegitimate tones, the little use of the five rhythm instruments, and the style of singing that lets you hear all consonants and no vowels.'[83] Yet Lombardo broke attendance records for black dancers at the Savoy Ballroom in Harlem. Louis's 1933 band used to run off the stand at the end of a set to listen to him on the radio, and Louis himself not only picked one of his records on the BBC's 'Desert Island Discs', but told another interviewer: *That band plays the tune, they put the melody there and it's beautiful. You can't find another band that can play a straight lead and make it sound that good.*[84] Although the Lombardo band was not exciting, or even interesting, it was certainly musical, which is not always true of the sounds people use for dancing.

In a decade of crazes in America, crazes for the blues, crosswords, mah-jong, flagpole-sitting and the Charleston, the craziest obsession of them all was the Big Bull Market, which began on 3 March 1928, spiralled upwards until it peaked on 3 September 1929 and crashed over October and November, cutting in half the value of the leading stocks, wiping out the savings of the small investors who thought it would never end, and ushering in the Great Depression which had been waiting in the wings. The writing was on the wall for Harlem's days of prosperity and Connie Immerman, who ran Connie's Inn, fired the band after persistent lateness by 'the lushies', as Louis contemptuously called the musicians who drank alcohol, rather than smoked pot. The band broke up, leaving Armstrong to work as a single, and he remembered a friend who worked on the railroad from New York to California, told him how popular he was there, and said he could get him a pass. Whether or not he travelled free, Armstrong arrived at Union Station in Los Angeles, found himself a room at the Dunbar Hotel on Central Avenue, the main street of the black entertainment district, and started looking for work. He soon found it in front of the band at Frank Sebastian's New Cotton Club, next to the MGM studios in Culver City, and a magnet for the Hollywood set.

Armstrong's first recording in California, in July 1930, was as accompanist to Jimmie Rodgers, the Singing Brakeman, a white pioneer of country and western music. On paper 'Blue Yodel No. 9' seems to be an unlikely meeting: in fact, Armstrong's muted obbligato fits evocatively with the dark little tale of street life in Memphis, Tennessee: it's a bit like a film-noir soundtrack. Rodgers has a more primitive approach than the vaudeville blues singers he was used to recording with, but Armstrong sails through his out-of-metre singing and yodelling, giving the performance an intense blues feeling. Five days later Armstrong was recording again, with the band from the club. It included two young men who would become jazz stars. The drummer was Lionel Hampton: in a few months Armstrong would spot a vibraphone in the studio and ask him to play it on 'Memories of You', so encouraging him to switch to the new instrument. As a result Hampton became a member of the Benny Goodman Quartet and eventually a bandleader in his own right. The trombonist was Lawrence Brown, who would be one of the longest-serving soloists in Duke Ellington's band. On their first record together, Brown takes an opening solo, Louis sings 'I'm a Ding Dong Daddy from Dumas', and then quickly moves off into scat, making the excuse that *I done forgot the words*. The vocal leads into an extended trumpet solo over a charging band, and near the end is the phrase which, a dozen years later, Louis's adversary and admirer Dizzy Gillespie would turn into 'Salt Peanuts'.

The same session produced 'I'm in the Market for You', in which the saxophones try to emulate Guy Lombardo's syrupy sound, but succeed only in producing an out-of-tune scramble. Louis tries to escape from the lyrics about brokers and shares, perhaps feeling that they are unlikely to please post-crash audiences. Although the saxophones are still floundering, he sounds happier with 'I'm Confessin'', and it marks the beginning of a two-year period during which OKeh recorded him in first-class new songs, the best that the finest composers of Broadway and Tin Pan Alley could provide. They included Johnny Green's 'Body and Soul', Fred Ahlert's 'Love, You Funny Thing!' and 'Walkin' My Baby Back Home', Walter Donaldson's 'You're Drivin' Me Crazy', and George Gershwin's 'I Got Rhythm', a tune based on harmonies which hundreds of jazz musicians have used for their own tunes since.

He did not treat any of them with exaggerated respect. But the most surprising performance is of a Hoagy Carmichael song, 'Star Dust', which had been around for five or six years, starting off as a tango, turning into a jazz tune, and picking up at least two sets of lyrics on the way.[85] Finally the bandleader Isham Jones recorded it as an emotional instrumental, showing the way everyone would treat it from then on. Bing Crosby made the first vocal record in August 1931, and Armstrong followed in November. His version of 'Star Dust' dispenses with the slightly operatic verse: after a band introduction he plays the chorus on the trumpet, pushing and pulling the phrases into a passionate restatement. He sings the whole first line of his vocal on one repeated note and the words merge with each other into a stream-of-consciousness meditation on 'memory'. The composer Alec Wilder pointed out that Carmichael's original melodic line 'is not, in the pure sense of the word, vocal'[86] and shows its instrumental origins: Armstrong's treatment of it seems to recognise that and find a new line suitable for singing. Because 'Star Dust' is so well known and admired, Armstrong's re-composing of it makes a clear example of how he could build a jazz performance out of high-quality raw materials, and enhance them by creating an overwhelmingly moving experience.

By the time he recorded 'Star Dust' Armstrong was back in Chicago, after the law caught up with him and his 'muggles'. One night, between sets at the Cotton Club, Armstrong had gone for a smoke with Vic Berton, a white drummer from Chicago who had begun a new career in the Hollywood studios at the birth of the talkies, and was playing with the Abe Lyman band at the Coconut Grove nightclub. Berton's brother Ralph told what happened: 'Vic had a whole can of new Mexican leaf he was going to lay on Louie. They were sitting in Louie's car, smoking a joint and rolling some more, when The Man came up behind them and flashed a light into the car, and a badge, and that was it.'[87]

Two detectives – aka The Man – arrested the two musicians and they spent a cheerful night in the cells, still high, until the next morning, when they found out that they could be fined $1,000 and jailed for six months. Fortunately, somebody stepped in and fixed the judge. According to Ralph Berton it was Lyman's brother, a power in local Democrat politics, who arranged for Armstrong and Vic Berton to serve their sentences by spending five nights a week in private rooms at a prison hospital for a time. Other versions say the fixer was an envoy from Tommy Rockwell, an ugly customer called Johnny Collins.

A podgy, fortyish man with a toothbrush moustache, Collins was said to be a lawyer and was certainly a crook. Yet Armstrong, perhaps grateful for being sprung, made him his manager, although he already had a contract with Rockwell. Armstrong's arrangements with women were complicated, too. Lil had arrived in Los Angeles with her masseur, who was supposed to stop her hips getting too large. *As if I didn't know her hips are sure to ignite from the friction,* Louis wrote. *Later on, I found out that this guy and*

Lil had been going together and he'd been spending my money for years. Then Alpha said she was so blue from thinking about me, and missed me so terribly much, that she boarded a train for California.[88] Armstrong found her a room, until the Cotton Club engagement ended and he had made his first film, providing music for a feature called 'Ex-Flame', which has been lost. Everybody went back to Chicago, Alpha to her mother's apartment and Armstrong to Lil's house. But he soon separated from Lil, although she would not give him a divorce.

Collins booked Armstrong into a downtown nightclub, the Showboat, and saxophonist Al Washington pulled together a nine-piece band which trumpeter Zilner Randolph rehearsed, though not too thoroughly, to

Prohibition gave America's criminals a licence to print money and a motive to organise when it was imposed throughout the nation in January 1920. It soon became clear that the federal government had neither the will nor the means to enforce a law which most urban adults found ridiculous and had no intention of obeying. With the public forced to be outlaws, the gangsters had a majority on their side. Speakeasies proliferated and cabarets where alcohol could not be sold openly charged extortionate prices for 'set-ups' – bottles of soda-water and ice so that customers could mix their own drinks with whatever they had in their hip-flasks. If they did not own the nightclubs, the Mob leeched cash from their proprietors through protection rackets. With nowhere else to work in those days before jazz came into the concert hall, musicians were inevitably caught up in the gangsters' web.

judge by their messy performances on the records Armstrong made with them. He demonstrates, not for the first or last time, a heroic ability to play at his best despite the out-of-tune saxophones and the unstable rhythm section. And his own opinion was clear: *Now there's a band that deserved a whole lot of credit that they didn't get. They made some of my finest recordings with me.*[89] George James, who played alto saxophone in the band, said it would open each half-hour set for ten minutes before bringing Louis on to the stand. 'Louis was supposed to do 20 minutes, but it wasn't always that way. We never knew how long he would stay out there because he was a showman. He played 100 per cent to his audience (so did we, for that matter). If the audience was hot, Louis would stay on as long as 30 or even 45 minutes. Some nights he was so eager he would come out before our ten minutes was up! When he was on stage, it was all Louis Armstrong, naturally – playing, singing, mugging, joking, dancing.[90]

Armstrong was pleased with business at the Showboat. But Collins and Rockwell were tussling over his contract, and he found himself in the middle of a gangland dispute. Two hoodlums tried to extort money from him, and one night some gangsters staged a fight on the dance floor while he was playing. On another evening he got a message on the stand that someone was waiting for him in his dressing room, and he found a bearded white man waiting there. The man pulled out a gun, gave his name as Frankie Foster, and said he had come to make sure Armstrong was on the morning train to New York to open at Connie's Inn. *Then he flashed his big ol' pistol and aimed it straight at me. With my eyes as big as saucers and frightened too, I said: 'Well, maybe I am going to New York.' Ooh God.* Foster led him at gunpoint to a telephone booth: *Sure enough, someone said hello, a familiar voice, too – yes, sir – I know that voice if I heard it a hundred years from now. The first words he said to me was: 'When are you gonna open here?' I turned and looked direct into Frankie Foster's face and said: 'Tomorrow a.m.'*[91]

Armstrong never revealed whose voice he recognised on the phone – suggestions include Rockwell, Connie Immerman and the rival Mob bosses, Owney Madden and Dutch Schultz – but he did not get on the train to New York. *I thought it best to leave town next morning,*[92] he explained. Collins got him away somehow, while McKendrick called the band together and swore them to secrecy. The band left town, too. Reunited with Armstrong, they began a journey through America in the grip of the Depression.

On the eve of the 1931 Kentucky Derby, the Armstrong band became the first black orchestra to play the Roof Garden of the Kentucky Hotel in Louisville. It was also the first of a gruelling series of one-night stands and short residencies booked by Johnny Collins in Illinois, Ohio, Kentucky, Tennessee, Maryland, Michigan, Wisconsin and Minnesota. The band was avoiding Mob-owned venues in New York and Chicago: it had to visit Chicago to record, but it did not appear there on stage. In June, for the first time in nine years, Louis went back to his home town, New Orleans.

He and the band travelled there in a private carriage on the L & N, the Louisville and Nashville railroad. George James described their reception. 'When we pulled into New Orleans, I couldn't believe my eyes. They had Canal Street all lit up, with crowds, and marching bands, and balloons, and so forth, like Mardi Gras.'[93]

My, it is a wonderful feeling to go back to your home town and find that while you have been away you have become a big man.[94]

The band members were well treated when they began their three-month residency outside the town at the Suburban Gardens, an expensive supper and gambling club with a gourmet kitchen: they could take their pick from the menu. 'It was a white club, so there was no coloured clientèle, but that

Throughout his career Armstrong used the 'pressure method' of playing the trumpet, building up breath in the air spaces of the head and forcing it into the instrument. The method damaged his lip, and can have other serious consequences for players' health, according to Gavin Henderson, the trumpeter who is Principal of Trinity College of Music, London. 'Modern brass playing is non-pressure playing: Wynton Marsalis is a non-pressure player. Most orchestral and brass band players tend to play the non-pressure method. You can go on for hours, but the heroic sound, the Jericho sound that you expect from the trumpet, comes from pressure playing.'[95]

didn't stop them listening to our orchestra. Our people would sit outside the club, on park benches along the riverfront, and listen to us through the open windows. Families would bring a picnic supper.'[96] But opening night presented a difficulty. The local radio station, WSMB, broadcast shows from the club 'live' – an important publicity role for touring bands. The announcer declared: 'I haven't the heart to announce the nigger on the radio.' Armstrong called for a chord from the band, strode to the microphone, and announced himself.

Off stage, he moved into an apartment with Alpha, visited the Waif's Home and handed out radios, bought uniforms for a baseball team attached to his old neighbourhood's burial society, the Zulu Social Aid and Pleasure Club, and had a cigar named after him, the Louis Armstrong Special.

Yet the visit ended badly. Armstrong had agreed to give a free performance for African Americans at an army base. Hundreds of people appeared, but they and the band were locked out: the army would not allow dancing on its land. Armstrong felt humiliated by this mean display of racist power, and promised to return.

At the Suburban Gardens: George James and Mike McKendrick are either side of Armstrong, Zilner Randolph is holding a trumpet in front of the bass

In 1935 he sneaked into town, played a week at a black theatre, and left again.

The 1931 tour ran into trouble at Memphis, Tennessee, when a white driver objected to the band boarding the bus they had hired to take them to the theatre where they were playing. Policemen were called, and were enraged when they saw Johnny Collins's white wife, who had been travelling with the band to help with travel arrangements, chatting with black men. They arrested everyone except the guitarist, Mike McKendrick, who saw what was happening and kept out of the way. While the rest of the band were locked up in jail, their lives threatened by the city's police, two thirds of whom were in the Ku Klux Klan, McKendrick located Collins, who got the theatre management to bail them out, on condition they make a broadcast. In front of the microphone next day, in a room full of police, Armstrong announced that he was dedicating the next number to the Memphis police force, and sang: 'I'll Be Glad When You're Dead, You Rascal, You.' When he came off the air, the police thanked him for the dedication.

The band toured theatres in the RKO circuit and the black TOBA circuit: the initials stood for Theatre Operators Booking Association, but musicians said they were Tough On Black Asses or, if they were being genteel, Artists.

In Philadelphia, Armstrong's lip began to give him trouble. 'First we noticed a blister on his chop, and every day it got worse until he couldn't put his mouthpiece on it,' said George James.

Even in the Depression year of 1932, the lowest point of record sales between 1920 and 1940, the recording industry survived with sales of six million records.[97]

'Louis could sing and joke around, but he simply couldn't play for a few days until his chops healed.'[98]

At last Collins accepted a booking in a Broadway theatre, but the Harlem club-owner Connie Immerman and Armstrong's ex-manager Tommy Rockwell sued for breach of contract, and the date was cancelled. The band broke up and Armstrong, after a brief return to California and the New Cotton Club, set sail for England. He and Collins may have been under the mistaken impression that there was no Depression in Europe.

Armstrong sailed on the *SS Majestic* with Alpha and the Collinses, landing in England on 14 July 1932. *An Englishman who met me at the boat in 1932, when I first went to England (we landed in Plymouth), he shook my hand saying 'Hello Satchmo.' Man, I flipped. That was my first time hearing this name . . . and I've been Satchmo ever since.*[99] The Englishman was Percy Brooks, editor of the popular-music paper, *Melody Maker*, and he may have simply mispronounced 'Satchelmouth', but the new name seems to have given Armstrong genuine pleasure, and he used it with relish in his announcements for the rest of his career.

In four days he was due to start a two-week booking at the London Palladium, the most important variety theatre in Britain, and he had no band. A message to Paris rounded up some of the expatriate African-Americans working there, and they were supplemented by a couple of London musicians. They may not have had much time for rehearsal and contemporary accounts suggest that the band was ragged. The critic Max Jones, writing long afterwards about a performance he saw at the age of 24, could not be sure: 'What I can call to mind is an image of the man out front – a lithe, smallish but power-packed figure prowling the stage restlessly, menacingly almost, and growling and gesticulating when he was not playing, singing or talking into the microphone. He addressed his trumpet as if it had life of its own (*Speak to 'em, Satchmouth*), and controlled the band with faintly alien suggestions like *Way down, way down, Keep muggin' . . . lightly, lightly and politely,* and *Swing, swing, swing, you cats.*'[100] Plunged into this as part of an evening of variety turns, some of the Palladium audience were baffled and upset: the trumpeter

Nat Gonella recalled tripping up people who were leaving during Armstrong's act. But at the end of the fortnight there were bookings in the provinces. The first band went back to Paris and a pianist, Billy Mason, assembled a band from the cream of London musicians for a tour which lasted until October. After a week's holiday in Paris, Armstrong and Alpha sailed home.

Collins, in spite of an existing contract with OKeh, signed a new one with Victor, and Armstrong began recording with other leaders' bands. His technique was at its peak, his sound at its most glowing. At the deepest point of the Depression, when thousands of men were scrambling on board freight trains in desperate search of work, Armstrong produced one of his most noble, triumphant solos on a piece credited to him as composer, 'Hobo, You Can't Ride This Train.' He sings the message in the character of the brakeman, the person the hobo most feared: 'One conductor might amiably let him ride, the next try to squeeze out of him a token fare for his own pocket or toss him overboard or bring in the cops.'[101] In the end, while the drummer Chick Webb makes train noises with his wire brushes, Armstrong, as amiable as ever, relents and says: *You're all right with me, I think I will let you ride.* Soon he got Zilner Randolph to form a band of enthusiastic youngsters, some of whom were to become important players. Saxophonists Scoville Browne and Budd Johnson, Budd's trombonist brother Keg and the pianist Teddy Wilson, later to make the greatest of Billie Holiday's records. Wilson said: 'Working with Armstrong and hearing him take a popular song and bring it to life and make a masterpiece out of it, night after night without fail, was one of the most marvellous things I've ever heard. The quality of the band behind him was no good at all, although we had some good soloists: the Johnson brothers were outstanding. But that was not too important as we played mainly background.'[102] For most of 'Laughin' Louie' the band doesn't even do that: there is a lot of laughter and a lot of silence until Louis suddenly produces a dancing unaccompanied cadenza. Budd Johnson's explanation was that Louis wanted everyone to get high before the recording. Budd took a vocal of his own on 'Sweet Sue' in a kind of pig Latin which Louis announces as *vipers' language* – a viper being musicians' slang for a pot-smoker. But aside from relaxing, the band was also able to provide support for dazzling new solos on 'Basin Street Blues' and 'Mahogany Hall Stomp'.

Yet for much of this time Armstrong had trouble with his upper lip. Mezz Mezzrow, travelling with him and presumably using his pot-procuring talents to keep the vipers high and happy, said: 'It was so bad, all raw and swole up, that he just sat and looked at it all day in a mirror, all the time applying some lip salve for trumpet players that Vincent Bach had put on the market, so it wouldn't be agony for him every time he blew into his horn. To make things worse, he kept picking at it with a needle.'[103] It wasn't as bad as the London *Daily Express* claimed in a story headlined 'Man With Iron Lips Killed By His Art' which said that he had 'died suddenly in a nursing home in New York, a victim to the terrific strain which his art put on him'.[104] More prosaically the British musician, Spike Hughes, on a visit to New York, told *Melody Maker* that Armstrong had been bitten by a dog, but that wasn't news.

Armstrong may have been in real danger later when two gangsters appeared in his dressing room in the Earle Theater in Philadelphia to 'protect' him when the manager paid him off. *I laid some jive talk on my valet. I knew they wouldn't understand it, but of course he did. He went out to the front of the house, collected my money and took it right to the bank.*[105] He played his last show, left by the stage door, and had himself locked up in a police cell. Then he and Collins went back to England on board the SS *Homeric*. A fellow-traveller was John Hammond, a 22-year-old Yale dropout just getting started in jazz journalism and record-producing. 'With Louis was his manager, Johnny Collins, a man I disliked. One night he got very drunk in Armstrong's stateroom while I was upbraiding him for using the word "nigger" and for his shabby treatment of Armstrong, who was, after all, Collins' bread and butter. The manager became so furious he took a swing at me. Somehow, for I certainly am no fighter, I managed to counter his punch and knock him on his behind. I think Louis never forgot that fight. It was probably the first time a white man had thought enough of him to fight someone who abused him.'[106] Collins was also suspected of under-paying Armstrong and his bandsmen, and then went back to the United States, taking Armstrong's passport with him. Armstrong, already launched on a tour with a similar band to the one hired in Paris, persuaded the British bandleader and impresario Jack Hylton to take over his management: Hylton booked the Armstrong band on a tour of Scandinavia, and part of the stage act was filmed in Copenhagen (and used in the Ken Burns documentary 'Jazz'). Armstrong took Alpha on holiday to Paris and found a new manager, N J Canetti. He toured Belgium and played concerts in Paris, where, in November 1934, the band recorded a double-sided 'On the Sunny Side of the Street', with masterly Armstrong contributions and the worst saxophones yet; a rhapsodic and wordless 'Song of the Vipers', and frenetic versions of 'St Louis Blues' and 'Tiger Rag' in which Armstrong's embouchure shows no sign of strain in the high notes. But a further tour through France, Switzerland and Italy ended in Turin, with Louis complaining that his lip was too badly damaged to go on. Under doctor's orders to rest it for six months, he went back to Chicago, and made a bargain with Joe Glaser.

Most people who knew Joe Glaser thought he was odious, even disgusting. Louis Armstrong loved him. Their partnership made them both millionaires, and Armstrong put its success down to the way Glaser had acted as the protector Black Benny Williams, his New Orleans mentor, had predicted he would need: *Dipper, as long as you live, no matter where you may be, always have a white man who like you and can & will put his hand on your shoulder and say, 'This is my nigger' – and can't nobody harm you.*[107]

Duke Ellington wrote perceptively of their relationship in his memoirs. 'Louis Armstrong and Joe Glaser; Joe Glaser and Louis Armstrong. Don't put the cart before the horse, they say, and at first glance you might think Louis was the horse doing all the pulling while Glaser was in the driver's seat of the cart. Obviously, a cart is a more convenient place to stash the gold. Then you realise that in spite of how well Joe Glaser did for himself, Louis still ended up a very rich man, maybe the richest of the "Trumpet Gabriels". This is not a fact to be ignored, for what more can one man do for another: Joe Glaser watched over Louis like the treasure he was, and saw to it that his partner was well fixed for the rest of his life.'[108]

Glaser was an unlikely guardian angel, his parents, who lived comfortable middle-class lives on Chicago's North Side, wanted him to follow his father and become a doctor. Instead Glaser dived into the Chicago underworld of the South Side, where his mother had invested in property and where southern African-Americans had formed the biggest black community in the United States. It was not surprising, in the Prohibition era, when he first met Armstrong, that he should be arrested for selling bootleg liquor and denounced in the press for bribing the police. Glaser himself never drank or smoked. But he was convicted of running a brothel and accused of raping one of its girls, a 14-year-old. He was sentenced to ten years, but the best legal brains in the Al Capone syndicate kept him out of prison by getting him to marry the girl. (They soon parted and some time later a pianist visiting Cleveland, Ohio, found her running a brothel with a good kosher kitchen.) A few weeks later, in March 1928, Glaser was accused of trying to rape a 17-year-old, but lawyers got him loose again. He was a rough man in a tough business, foul-mouthed, evil-tempered and impossible to beat in a bargain. He carried two rolls of money in the pockets of his sharply tailored suits, ready to hand out to performers who approached him with hard-luck stories: those whom Glaser judged likely to be washed up got a two-dollar bill from one roll, those who might claw their way back to the top got a twenty-dollar bill from the other.

Charlie Holmes, the alto-player who would work with Armstrong after Louis took over Luis Russell's band, offered an explanation for the bizarre and contradictory behaviour: 'Joe Glaser was a funny person. He was shell-shocked in the first war. He'd get to hollering and screaming at Luis Russell, you could hear him all over the theatre, but next day he'd go out and buy Luis Russell a great big fancy wardrobe trunk, something expensive.'[109]

When Armstrong returned to Chicago Glaser was flat broke: one story was that he had offended a Mob leader, fled to Paris, and fallen on hard times when his parents died. The promoter Ernie Anderson recalled Armstrong telling him how he asked Glaser to be his manager: '*You collect the money. You pay me one thousand dollars every week free and clear. You pay off the band, the travel and hotel expenses, my income tax, and you take everything that's left.* They shook hands on this arrangement. There was no other contract.'[110]

Glaser's business expanded into the Associated Booking Corporation (he chose the initials to be near the front of the phone book, and then worked out a name to fit them). His client list grew to include Billie Holiday, Ella Fitzgerald, Pearl Bailey, Duke Ellington, Dinah Washington, Sarah Vaughan, and later Lionel Hampton. Seeing his success, white artists joined as well: Noel Coward, Gene Krupa, and later George Shearing and Barbra Streisand.

Glaser's version was that when Armstrong came back from Europe, 'he was broke and very sick. He said, *I don't want to be with nobody but you. Please, Mr Glaser, just you and I. You understand me, I understand you.* And I said, "Louis, you're me and I'm you." I insured his life and mine for $100,000 apiece. Louis didn't even know it. I gave up all my other business and we went on the road together.'[111]

Armstrong wrote later that their relationship dated back to the Sunset Café: *I always admired Mr Glaser from the first day I started working for him. He just impressed me different from the other bosses I've worked for. He seemed to understand coloured people so much.*[112] He may have decided that Glaser's personality was no worse than Collins's, and Glaser was certainly right that Armstrong was in financial difficulty: his career was stalled by the lay-off enforced by his lip trouble and by the disputes between the various managers, promoters and record companies who believed he owed them something, and had lawyers to back their claims. On top of that Lil was suing for $6,000 in unpaid maintenance. Glaser extricated him from the money problems: some claimants were paid off, some squared, some were ignored. With his embouchure recovered, Armstrong asked Zilner Randolph to form another band for him. When it set out in July 1935 for a tour, the bus driver was white, to minimise harassment in the southern states. Glaser rode along as well.

Although most black performers had white management, because white theatre owners and promoters would not deal with blacks, it was unusual for a white manager to travel with a band. The commitment to Armstrong which this showed impressed the black entertainment community. It laid the foundations of the management firm Glaser set up in New York. African-Americans wanted to be represented by him. But some later regretted having come under his control, and felt they were second-class clients compared to Armstrong. Lionel Hampton complained at the long distances between his band's jobs: 'Joe Glaser said we could make more money in four weeks in four different cities than we could playing a month in the same place. He was right, but he never stopped to consider that the gigs he set up with a phone call meant miles and miles of travel for us.'[113] The trumpet-players in particular felt they had a raw deal: Roy Eldridge said about the later 30s: 'Glaser signed both me and Hot Lips Page, but I swear he did it to keep us under wraps and away from Louis, who was having a little lip trouble then.'[114] Eldridge also said that Glaser forced him to join his agency by buying his contract from a former agent.

Glaser made a habit of attending black theatres and dance halls and talking on an equal footing to black artists. But Ernie Anderson, who disliked Glaser, claimed to have learned his real opinion when he encountered him alone one night and asked after Louis. 'These shines are all alike,' Glaser said. 'They're so lazy. You know that don't you?'[115]

Glaser controlled Armstrong's professional life for 34 years, booking dates, agreeing fees and dictating publicity. He even decided who would be in the band and what tunes he would play.

Armstrong was free to concentrate on his performance, unencumbered by the administrative details that assail the average bandleader before he can walk on to the stage. He was even willing to let Glaser to run aspects of his private life, though he never let Glaser's disapproval of drugs put him off marijuana. In return for a percentage of his fees which is still mysterious, Glaser raised Louis from accompanying dancers to playing in theatres, from making records for other African-Americans to having a global audience, from nightclub entertainer to Hollywood actor. He made Louis Armstrong into a star.

One early result of the pact with Joe Glaser was a new recording contract. Glaser made a deal with Jack Kapp, a former employee of the collapsed Brunswick record label. He had hit on the idea that during a Depression you were more likely to sell records at 35 cents than at 75 cents. In 1934 he set up an American subsidiary of Decca, a new British record company in desperate need of new songs from the States. Kapp began to recruit performers, many of whom had been recording for small labels driven out of business by the hard times. His first signings were Guy Lombardo and Bing Crosby, who was getting exposure on stage, radio and films. Armstrong, on the other hand, had been abroad and out of sight.

Along with the new record label he got a new band to call his own, although in fact it belonged to the pianist and arranger Luis Russell, who continued to lead it while Armstrong stood in front. Russell had had a series of hits – all of the same tune, 'Call of the Freaks', under different titles – in the late 20s and early 30s, but he was out of fashion and needed work. Though the band was no longer at its superb best, the musicians were skilled, and its nucleus was a powerhouse New Orleans rhythm section built around Paul Barbarin's propulsive drums, Pops Foster's string bass, bowed, plucked or slapped – and Russell's *good New Orleans piano, very lusty and swingy*,[116] as Armstrong described it, though the records do not bear him out.

Russell and Glaser gradually strengthened the band, mostly by re-hiring former members. When Armstrong took it over, its outstanding soloist was Charlie Holmes, an alto saxophonist who grew up in Boston, Mass., with Johnny Hodges, the star of the Duke Ellington orchestra, and had a similarly elegant style. He was joined by the exuberant trombonist J C Higginbotham, the great New Orleans clarinet-player Albert Nicholas and the trumpeter Henry 'Red' Allen, from Algiers, on the other side of the Mississippi, who had marched beside Armstrong in the Allen Brass Band, led by his cornet-player father, Henry, Sr., some years before.

Luis Russell (1902–63) was born in Panama and as a teenager played piano in a cinema until he won $3,000 in a lottery and moved to New Orleans and then Chicago, working with King Oliver there and in New York. Russell formed a band, which started making joyous, romping records in 1929, when it also backed Armstrong in the studio. In 1943 Russell started his own band again, but left full-time playing five years later to teach and run a sweetshop. By the early 1960s he was working as a chauffeur.

'Red' Allen was one of the few trumpeters who could be taken seriously as a rival to Armstrong, and Glaser scored a coup by bringing him into the band. Not only did he control the competition, he also secured a strong soloist with an individual style who could help to build up the audience's excitement before Armstrong came on stage for his feature numbers, and who could carry the show if Armstrong's lip let him down. Glaser 'was shrewd enough to know that if Louis continued to spend hours each night blowing powerful high notes he might well inflict permanent damage on his lips'.[117] So Allen became Glaser's insurance policy. He does not seem to have resented the fact that he recorded no solos with the band: 'It was no fault of Louis', and I played plenty on the stand.'[118]

In 1936 Armstrong wrote in praise of the orchestra: *When I am swingin' trumpet out in front of them, with my back to them, I always know that however far I swing away from the music we are playing, wherever the music carries them, they will be right in there following close, hot and sure of their rhythm, and never losing their way for one second.*[119] Charlie Holmes remembered the demands Armstrong would make: 'We were blowing on a broadcast and somebody walked by and requested a number, and Louis turned to the band and was going to start straight into it. Well, you just don't do that on a broadcast. He didn't care. He just loved to blow. He's the greatest.'[120]

The collaboration started uncertainly, the saxophones sounding lacklustre as they struggled to emulate Armstrong's beloved Lombardo sound on 'Thanks a Million' and 'Red Sails in the Sunset'. But even before the recruitment drive for front-line players, the band had supported Louis in one of his most memorable performances in May 1936. 'Swing That Music' is a rarity among Armstrong records, an example of what used to be called a 'killer-diller' – an up-tempo number designed to rouse the audience to a frenzy.

The tune is a simple one, based on a repeated five-note phrase, and Pops Foster's slapped bass sets the band pounding in the old Russell style. Armstrong's vocal is slightly breathless, adding to the excitement, and then the saxophones leap hungrily on an arranged passage. Armstrong, using his well-tried methods of long notes and repetition, winds up the tension in three powerful choruses, and then delivers the knock-out punch: a final chorus consisting of no fewer than 42 high Cs, topped off with a devastating E flat. The wonder of it is that he constantly varies the rhythm so that each C seems to make a separate musical point, preventing the performance from being merely a vir-

Swing is a quality most jazz has to some extent, the result of a steady pulse with one or more counter-rhythms going on at the same time, so that the listener enjoys the tension between the two. In the 30s the word came to mean the big-band music popular at the time.

tuoso display — and he could not pull off the feat without the enthusiastic but accurate support of the band. Indeed, it is possible that he never tried it again: three months later he recorded 'Swing That Music' with Jimmy Dorsey's band in Los Angeles: they play beautifully for him, and execute a saxophone passage with textbook precision and great fire, but his solo is shorn of the final chorus, and it stayed that way on all the recordings until the end of the 40s, when it seems to have dropped out of his repertoire.

Another 'Swing That Music' appeared in November 1936: it was Armstrong's first book. The tune was written to publicise the book rather than the book being titled to exploit a hit number. A song copy and solos transcribed from performances by Armstrong and other star soloists formed an appendix. The publisher was clearly aiming at a growing market of white kids caught up in the latest craze sweeping America — the swing bands. All the soloists except Armstrong and the pianist-bandleader Claude Hopkins are white, the introduction is by crooner-bandleader Rudy Vallée, and the text makes Armstrong seem a big fan of the Original Dixieland Jazz Band. Nevertheless, it contains the bones of a history of jazz, something that did not exist in book form at the time, along with a first 'Autobiography' and some polemic on behalf of swing. Armstrong has clearly contributed, but there is a ghost present, presumably Horace Gerlach, who is credited as co-writer of the song and editor of the 'music section'. This is supposedly a technical exposition but is largely gobbledygook. The jazz scholar Dan Morgenstern excuses him: 'Gerlach undoubtedly meant well, and in 1936 he was only 25, clearly caught up in the budding swing craze of which this book was a product.'[121]

Jazz mythology dates the beginning of the swing era to the night of 21 August 1935, when Benny Goodman's band, dispirited after an unsuccessful tour across from the East Coast, opened at the Palomar ballroom in Los Angeles. Goodman threw caution and his arrangements of pop songs to the wind and played some of the scores he had bought from Fletcher Henderson, thus discovering that a young audience had heard that brand of hot big-band music on records and radio – Goodman had been playing the Henderson book in the two hours of his show which were broadcast to the West Coast after New York station executives had tucked themselves up in bed. Suddenly everyone wanted swing bands and jazz started its period of being the popular music of America and most of Europe. The story was not really so simple: Henderson was among a number of arrangers developing the four-in-a-bar style which Armstrong had pioneered. In fact, swing band popularity had been building up for several years among college kids and other young people who had access to records of black artists, particularly Armstrong, who was selling 100,000 records a year even in the Depression. The Palomar was just the place where the pressure exploded and the music flooded over the adult population.

Armstrong's rhythmic innovations were the essence of swing, and his band contained musicians flexible enough to fit in with the new fashion. 'Satchel Mouth Swing', for instance (a version of 'Coal Cart Blues' with different, Armstrong-oriented, lyrics) emphasises the orchestra, with the tune being introduced by the band and no solo from Armstrong until right at the end, after his vocal and solos by Holmes and Higginbotham. A new 'Struttin' with Some Barbecue' from the same 1938 session pits Louis against a background of riffs instead of a saxophone choir of the Lombardo stamp, and culminates in an indescribable piece of lip gymnastics. But that day's 'Jubilee' shows one of the band's limitations: Paul Barbarin, the stalwart of the New Orleans streets, tends to thrash and thump the drums in climaxes, perhaps trying to emulate Goodman's star drummer,

'Sid's personality reflected his playing. He was lovable and loving. He was gentle. He was compassionate and concerned. He was also vulnerable.'[122]

–Mel Powell

Gene Krupa. He breaks the flow, and sounds old-fashioned for the job in hand. Within a year he had been replaced by Big Sid Catlett, who has a claim to be called the greatest drummer jazz has ever seen.

Catlett was capable, he declared, of swinging a 17-piece band with a single wire brush played on a telephone directory, and nobody has challenged the boast. He urged bands relentlessly but lightly forward, anticipating the beat so that he sometimes seemed to be speeding up – but wasn't. Detractors from the traditionalist school accused him of 'dropping bombs' because he used accents in unexpected places to create cross-rhythms – but the

Sidney Catlett (1910–51) 'has yet to be matched,' wrote the critic Whitney Balliett. 'He has outstripped two batches of pursuers – the drummers of his own generation or persuasion and the modernist drummers. And he has remained the Master.'[123] Born in Evansville, Indiana, and beginning his career in Chicago, Catlett recorded in 1933 in New York with Benny Carter and with the all-star band assembled for the British composer Spike Hughes. He joined Armstrong from Don Redman's band.

accents spurred soloists to new heights. With a sense of time as loose but faultless as Armstrong's, Catlett loped effortlessly through his performances, like a panther on steel springs. He is one of the handful of drummers whose solos are worth hearing: Ruby Braff, the great cornet-player, said 'Watching him take a solo was a thrill. He hypnotised you. His sticks went so fast that they were blurred. But they also looked like they were moving in slow motion.'[124] Catlett was 6ft. 3in. tall with shoulders to match, and strong enough to pick up taxi-drivers with one enormous hand. Admired and loved by everyone he knew, he regarded sleep as a waste of time.

He would spend the next ten years with Armstrong apart from four months in 1941 when he joined the Goodman band and an awe-inspiring rhythm section that included a genius of the electric guitar, Charlie Christian, and a brilliant young pianist, Mel Powell. They were not together long before tuberculosis forced Christian out, and Goodman, apparently scared by Catlett's talent and showmanship, fired him. He went back to Armstrong.

How Catlett revolutionised the band can be heard in his first recording session in 1939. He pads on those panther paws through 'Jeepers Creepers', and then, in 'What is This Thing Called Swing?' uses snare-drum rolls to bustle the band's various sections into high-speed passages of instrumental showing off (including a disciplined outburst of his own) before driving Armstrong's solo with a non-stop four-in-a-bar pounding on his bass drum and a surging pulse on his ride cymbal. By April the band had become a loose-limbed swing team: even the Lombardo saxophones are almost house-trained for a remake of 'West End Blues' in which Armstrong rides into the coda over Catlett's relaxed beat. On 'Savoy Blues' and 'Heah Me Talkin' to Ya' Catlett uses an off-beat thwack to drive Armstrong's solos, prefiguring his later admirer, Art Blakey. The arrangements are improving, too, with more opportunities for solos by other band members and space for the sections to add colour; the character of the old Russell band has been lost, but however sophisticated and cohesive it became, nothing with Armstrong and Catlett in it could be called an ordinary swing band. The songs Armstrong recorded ranged, as usual, from silly novelty numbers through the day's pop tunes to revived blues and other *good ol' good ones*, as Armstrong called them. In 1938 he dug up a forgotten spiritual which had never been used in a jazz performance before, 'When the Saints Go Marching In.'

It was a hit, and perhaps an omen. The immediate impact was that Armstrong found himself in a New York studio with four 'spirituals' to record and a group of white singers pretending to be slaves on the old plantation: on 'Going to Shout All Over God's Heaven' the Lyn Murray Chorus 'intones, "hebbin, hebbin"; Armstrong growls right back at them, *heaven, heaven*.'[125] But his affinity with words, particularly unusual ones, makes him relish singing about Shadrack, Meshack and Abednego in Nebuchadnezzar's fiery furnace, and for 20 years or more he went on singing 'Shadrack', which is actually an imitation spiritual by a white man, Robert MacGimsey. The collaboration with the chorus was just one result of Jack Kapp's policy of shuffling his pack of Decca performers and dealing them out two at a time, so that Armstrong was paired not only with such obvious swing attractions as Jimmy Dorsey's orchestra and the Casa Loma Orchestra, but also with such unlikely partners as The Polynesians ('On a Coconut Island') and Andy Iona and his Islanders ('On a

From a small town in Ohio the Mills Brothers vocal quartet became international stars, capable of entertaining a popular audience while also showing 'not just driving power, but also the inventiveness expected of any self-respecting jazz musicians'.[127] By the time they worked with Armstrong one of the brothers had died and been replaced by his father. In 1943 their 'Paper Doll' sold six million records.

Little Bamboo Bridge'). *I have played with quite a few musicians who weren't so good,* he wrote later. *But as long as they could hold their instruments correct, and display their willingness to play as best they could, I would look over their shoulders and see Joe Oliver and several other great masters from my home town.*[126] So Armstrong often emerged well from these encounters, but never more successfully than from his meetings with the Mills Brothers.

Using nothing but their four voices and a single guitar, the brothers could outswing most 13-piece bands, and could even fool you into thinking they *were* a 13-piece band by imitating the sounds of instruments. Their timing meshed exactly with Armstrong's, and on 'Cherry' they even gave him a discreet version of the Lombardo saxophone sound without losing any of their momentum. The peculiar charm of the records they made together, fewer than a dozen, is that even in an out-and-out swinger like 'Flat Foot Floogie', the runaway novelty hit by Slim Gaillard, the fact that he was competing with only four voices meant that Louis had no need for grandstanding.

This intimate, chamber-music quality makes the Armstrong–Mills Brothers sides reminiscent of another unit which combined subdued dynamics with fierce swing, the John Kirby band. Critics have not dealt kindly with this sextet, which Kirby led from the double-bass: the complaint is that it diluted jazz by emphasising technical polish, virtuoso arrangements, and a library which plundered the out-of-copyright repertoire from Beethoven's Seventh Symphony to Scottish folk songs. There certainly is a cutesy-pie flavour to many Kirby records which suggests that he was playing jazz for people who don't like jazz; on the other hand there are inventive solos by trumpeter Charlie Shavers and pianist Billy Kyle. The band's first and biggest hit was a swing arrangement of 'Loch Lomond', recorded under the name of Kirby's wife, the innocent-sounding singer Maxine Sullivan, a tiny ball of fire who was still fizzing round the jazz festival circuit in the 1980s, practising her valve-trombone between appearances. In October 1937 she covered a song Louis had recorded with the Mills Brothers in April: 'Darling Nellie Gray'. You would never guess from either Sullivan's or Armstrong's version that the song is about slavery.

As the critic Gary Giddins has pointed out, it was written in the 1850s in support of the Abolitionist campaign. Nellie or Nelly Gray was literally sold down the river from her home in Kentucky just before she was due to marry. Benjamin Hanby, a white clergyman's son, heard her story and wrote the song. Many Americans of both races would know the verse which neither Armstrong nor Sullivan sings, including the words:

> *The white man bound her with his chain,*
> *They have taken her to Georgia*
> *For to wear her life away,*
> *As she toils in the cotton and the cane.*

The cut obscures the message, but there is no hiding the fact that on the other side of the Armstrong 78 is 'a nostalgic minstrel expression of mourning for the Old South, for massa and the plantation'.[128] The song is 'Carry Me Back to Old Virginny', written in 1878 by the black minstrel James Bland, whose home state was New York. Armstrong doesn't sing 'ol'massa'; he sings *old master*. He doesn't sing 'this old darkie's heart'; he sings *the old darkie's heart*. A couple of months later, recording 'Old Folks at Home', Stephen Foster's 1851 paean to the South, he subverts the song by allowing the Mills Brothers to do all the singing.

He urges them on as if they were in church, with a series of spoken remarks: *Hallelujah, Hallelujah! . . . Yowsah!* And so on, ending with *Well, looka here, we are far away from home . . . yeah, man.* He takes a similarly detached, ironic stance in one of the last Mills Brothers sides, in 1940, though we are no longer dealing with the South specifically, but the whole of Depression America. He talks through all but a dozen bars of his part in 'WPA', which pokes fun at the New Deal's Works Progress Administration through which the federal government financed jobs for 8,500,000 unemployed people mainly on building roads and other public projects. 'Can't get fired,' say the lyrics, 'so I take my rest until my work is through.' Washington objected and Decca withdrew the disc.

Armstrong was sometimes accused by younger African-Americans of being an 'Uncle Tom' – a label based on a misconception of Harriet Beecher Stowe's 1850s Abolitionist novel, *'Uncle Tom's Cabin'*. Armstrong was to prove them wrong in the 1950s by challenging the President of the United States on segregation, but it is unlikely that he felt his own position – or that of any other African-American – was secure enough during the Depression for him to declare outright opposition to racism. He also had a different sensitivity to language which later generations found offensive. In 'Black and Blue', the nearest he came to a racial protest, he went on singing the phrase *I'm white inside* – written by a black lyricist – from 1929 to the end of his career. Although he scrupulously avoided using pronunciations which fitted the stereotype of a black Southerner, the word 'darkies' seems to have not bothered him at all, however uncomfortable it made younger performers and audiences, and he made a joke in 'Just

'Today, Uncle Tom has become synonymous with the sycophant, fawning Negro, a characterization not intended by the author, nor was he seen as a figure of contempt by the black population of that era.'[129]

a Gigolo' by singing *just another jig I know*, abbreviating 'jig-gaboo', which one dictionary declares 'a slave term, it was always pejorative.'[130]

Armstrong was getting out of step musically, too, as the 1930s ended. Although big-band swing was still the dominant force in popular music, it was under fire from a growing group of jazz fans. The so-called New Orleans revival started with record collectors, who were listening to discs made in the early days of jazz and overturning what little was known of its history.

Enthusiasts found that many exponents of the New Orleans style Armstrong had left behind were living and performing in the city and willing to be interviewed and recorded. Others who had joined the migration north, such as Sidney Bechet and the trumpeter Tommy Ladnier, were brought into the studios to play in their original style.

White youngsters from San Francisco to Stockholm began to imitate what they heard on records and the radio. Jack Kapp, never slow to spot a trend, got Armstrong and the big band to re-record some tunes from the Hot Five era, including 'Savoy Blues' and 'West End Blues'. Then, in May 1940, with a pick-up band including Bechet, he recorded four tunes, including 'Coal Cart Blues' and 'Perdido Street Blues', for a Decca album of New Orleans-style jazz on 78s. The results are exciting, because both Armstrong and Bechet were in competitive mood. Bechet complained later that Armstrong changed his mind after the rehearsal and played something different for the recording. If that is true, then Bechet was ready for him and gave as good as he got. Bechet's judgement was: 'It seemed like he was wanting to make it a kind of thing where we were supposed to be bucking with each other, competing

'In 1935, the now-accepted classic items by the Louis Armstrong Hot Five and Hot Seven were dismissed as merely crude, and Jelly Roll Morton was a shadowy figure who had made a few obscure "race" records.'[131]

instead of working together for that real feeling that would let the music come new and strong.'[132]

The revival came too late for one of the New Orleans greats. One Thursday night in 1937, Armstrong and his band were in Savannah, Georgia, on their way to play a dance during a southern tour. Louis saw an old man stooped over a cart of vegetables and tapped him on the shoulder to get his attention. The man turned, and Louis found himself facing his mentor, King Oliver. A series of disasters culminating in a bus breakdown had stranded Oliver and his band in the South a year before, and he was still trying to work his way back to New York. Armstrong gave him about $150 he had in his pockets and took a whip-round from the band. That night he looked into the wings and saw that Oliver had got his clothes out of pawn, *Stetson hat turned down, high-button shoes, his box-back coat. He looked beautiful and he had a wonderful night, just listening to us – talking.*[133] The tour had to continue, leaving Oliver to save enough to get north. But not only were his teeth troubling him still, he also had high blood pressure and could not afford treatment. On 10 April 1938, King Oliver died alone in his room of a cerebral haemorrhage. His sister arranged for his body to be sent to New York in a cheap coffin. Armstrong played at his funeral.

When Alpha Smith, the girl Armstrong had spotted at the Vendome theater, threatened to sue him for breach of promise, he pleaded with Lil to keep their marriage going, even though it was years since they had lived together. 'I gave him the divorce just to spite him,' Lil said later,[134] so in October 1938 Armstrong had to marry Alpha, although a woman called Polly Jones was also claiming breach of promise. *A no-good bitch*[135] was Armstrong's judgement on his gold-digging third wife, who eventually ran off with Cliff Leeman, Artie Shaw's drummer. Armstrong had seen an attractive alternative a matter of weeks after the wedding, when he went to work at the new location of the Cotton Club, near

Times Square in midtown Manhattan. He worked there with the entertainer he most admired: Bill Robinson, the great tap-dancer and comedian who became a Broadway star at the age of 50 in 1929, after rescuing a feeble show from closure.

Robinson was already a vaudeville headliner when, seven years earlier, a tour brought him to Chicago. The young second cornet-player in King Oliver's band watched in awe from the audience as Robinson, dressed in a light tan suit *so sharp he was bleeding* stepped into a spotlight to start his act. *He waited after the thunderous applause had finished, and looked up into the booth and said to the man who controlled the lights – Bill said to him: 'Give me a light my colour.' And all the lights all over the house went out.*[136]

Bill Robinson (1878–1949) introduced a swinging style of tap-dancing on the toes; his virtuoso Stair Dance was seen in 'The Little Colonel', one of the Hollywood films in which he partnered the child star Shirley Temple. He had a reputation for being quarrelsome, and his nickname, Bojangles, was said to mean 'squabbler'.

At the Cotton Club there was a chorus line, and Armstrong noticed a girl known as Brown Sugar, whose real name was Lucille Wilson. She came from Corona, Queens, a suburb of New York near where La Guardia Airport is now, and was working as a dancer only because her middle-class family had been hit hard by the Depression. To make ends meet she brought home-made cookies to work with her, and toured the dressing rooms before show time to sell them to the cast. Armstrong helped her out by ordering her whole consignment every night, handing them out to Harlem children the next day. *She's doing her dance every night directly in front of me standing there directing the band and blowing my solos on my trumpet whenever it was time for me to blow and wail. All of those beautiful notes along with Lucille's perfect dancing. Me – digging those cute li'l buns of hers.*[137] At last, Louis said: *Lucille, I might as well tell you right now – I have eyes for you*, and although she just laughed, before long they were going to the movies together between shows,

Lucille Armstrong with Louis

and riding uptown to Harlem after work behind the chauffeur of Armstrong's rust-coloured Packard.

There were interruptions when the band went out of town, but on 2 October 1942, Armstrong was divorced from Alpha by a Chicago court and ten days later he and Lucille were married in St Louis. She returned to New York, he began a string of one-nighters and when it ended the following March he took a taxi to the three-storey house Lucille had bought for $3,900 in Corona. *One look at that big fine house, and right away I said to the driver 'Aw man, quit kidding.'*[138] Lucille let him in, and 34–56 107th Street was his home for the rest of his life.

Armstrong spent most of the year away on tour and Lucille liked to stay at home. That gave him what he saw as an excuse for having liaisons with other women, sometimes one-night stands, occasionally longer-running affairs. Apart from advising him to find a white protector, Black Benny Williams had told him: 'No matter how many times you get married, always have another woman for a sweetheart on the outside. Because "Mad Day" might come, or she could be the type of woman whose ego, after realising that you care deeply, may for no reason at all try giving you a hard time.'[139] Armstrong wrote in a 1955 letter to Glaser: *That's why I have several chicks that I enjoy whaling with the same as I do with Lucille. And she's always had the choicest ass of them all.*[140] One of them was a famous entertainer, a widow known to Armstrong as Sweets or Sweetie, who had taken part in a tour with him through Canada and the Midwest to Las Vegas. One night after a show in Montreal, Louis told Glaser, *I just kept laying those hot kisses up on her fine chops. When two people are in a room by themselves, kissing will lead to fucking every time.*[141] Armstrong's purpose in telling the story to Glaser was that he was about to set out on tour abroad and wanted to make sure that his manager would continue the payments he had been making to Sweets for a baby she said was his. The clarinet-player Barney Bigard, by that time a member of Armstrong's All Stars band, remembered Armstrong being proud of fathering a child, and trying to persuade Lucille that they ought to adopt the baby. 'Who told you you got a baby by Sweetie?' Lucille asked. 'She done fool you, and she's got a boyfriend. He must have done it, and he's telling her to tell you that you're the father. You sure are stupid.'[142] Armstrong had to be satisfied with continuing to care for his cousin Clarence. Jack Bradley, a distinguished jazz photographer and a close friend of Armstrong, often met Clarence in dressing rooms and nightclubs with Louis, who introduced him as *my adopted son Clarence*. 'I can't tell you how important he was to Louis,' said Bradley. 'He was retarded and an embarrassment to Glaser and Lucille, but Louis always welcomed him, and took care of him. He probably had the mind of a 10- or 12-year-old, but he was a beautiful guy. I strongly believe that Louis was

Armstrong and Martha Raye in 'Artists and Models'

Clarence's father.'[143] Bradley said that Armstrong had 'sort of bought' an older woman named Evelyn Hadfield to marry Clarence and look after him. When she died in the 1980s Clarence went into a care home in the Bronx and died on 27 August 1998. Bradley tried unsuccessfully to get him a grave next to Armstrong, and had him buried at his own expense in New Jersey.

Armstrong's career in movies had begun in 1931, about the same time as Robinson's; they were among the first black artists acceptable to Hollywood, which preferred white actors wearing burnt cork. Armstrong's appearances included being a disembodied live-action head singing 'I'll Be Glad When You're Dead, You Rascal You' in a Betty Boop cartoon, and a handful of 'soundies', four-minute films based on his records. His roles in feature pictures are generally excuses for letting him sing. Some of his stranger records are covers for songs he introduced on the screen: they include 'The Skeleton in the Closet' from 'Pennies From Heaven' with his friend and fan Bing Crosby, and 'The Trumpet Player's Lament', which was cut from release prints of 'Doctor Rhythm'. Producers discovered that his personality would help to bring in the crowds, but found it hard to handle the idea of an African-American star, particularly when there was a girl in the same scene. In 'Artists and Models', a song making a joke about the perils of jazz, 'Public Melody Number

'Louis was born black, but he didn't make a career of it. For that he was sometimes called an Uncle Tom. It really didn't bother him very much because Louis Armstrong was one of the natural wonders of the world.'
–Danny Kaye[144]

One', outraged the bigots because Louis sang it with Martha Raye, who danced a comic version of a woman driven crazy by rhythm.

Raye was in blackface, but the performance was too sexy for some of the people who knew she was white. So in 'Going Places', starring Dick Powell, the black actors were kept away from the whites. Armstrong won an Oscar nomination for singing a love song by Harry Warren and Johnny Mercer, which the composer Alec Wilder called 'a wonderful rhythm song, with an equally wonderful lyric . . . It begs no quarter, merely rolls up its sleeves and goes to work.'[145] The song has been remembered long after the now-forgotten film, so few people will know that Armstrong sang 'Jeepers Creepers' to a horse.

In spite of the indignities he endured from Hollywood, Armstrong's career was in good shape as the 1940s began and the Second World War brought economic expansion to the United States. His movie roles had made him acceptable to advertisers who might have been reluctant to use a black performer to appeal to white consumers, and he became the first African-American to make frequent broadcasts on radio shows with national sponsors. Glaser had put him on a sound footing – just in time.

Jack-Armstrong Blues

American music was thrown into turmoil on 1 August 1942 by a man who was, on his own admission, a poor performer. 'If I was a good trumpet-player I wouldn't be here,' said James Petrillo, President of the American Federation of Musicians (AFM). 'I got desperate. I hadda look for a job. I went in the union business.'[146]

Petrillo believed that records, played on the radio, the juke-box or at home, were depriving musicians of work by replacing live performers, and he called his members out on a strike against the record companies, trying to force them to pay into a union fund which would compensate unemployed players. The music historian Sigmund Spaeth called the demand 'absurd', and denounced it as 'exactly the same as having every brick-layer share in the rentals of any building he helped construct, or every type-setter collect a percentage of authors' royalties and publishers' profits on every book he helped put into print.'[147] Spaeth and the record companies argued that records helped to publicise bands and therefore brought work for musicians.

The ban means that there is a hole in the documents of jazz history: commercial recordings were not made, so the picture we have of a crucial time is incomplete. That records exist at all for the period of the ban – nearly two years – is due mainly to the fact that America was at war and needed to maintain the morale of its troops.

Performances by Armstrong with his touring big band, mainly broadcast from military bases, have been preserved on AFRS (Armed Forces Radio Service) transcriptions. But a new aspect to his career is documented on V-Discs, starting with an extraordinary night in January 1944, the first jazz concert at the Metropolitan Opera House. The musicians who performed had come top (or in some cases nearly top) of an *Esquire* magazine poll, not of readers but of jazz experts: it was a genuine all-star occasion, and Armstrong was joined in the front line by Roy Eldridge on trumpet, Jack Teagarden on trombone, Barney Bigard on clarinet (a deputy for the winner, Benny Goodman), Coleman Hawkins on tenor saxophone and Red Norvo on vibraphone. The singers were Billie Holiday and Mildred Bailey. The rhythm section brought together Armstrong's own drummer, Sid Catlett, with Fats Waller's guitarist, Al Casey, the brilliant young bassist Oscar Pettiford and the virtuoso pianist Art Tatum, who was better known as a solo performer and leader of a trio than as part of an informal band. But he clearly relishes the work, and the surging drive the rhythm section creates is so intense that on 'I Got Rhythm' Armstrong cannot restrain himself and leaps into his solo almost before Norvo has finished his. The jam session format seems to have enlivened Armstrong, and he turned up at a V-Disc session where he was not expected: Jack Teagarden's delighted vocal on 'Play Me the Blues' (also called 'Jack-Armstrong Blues') shows his surprise at seeing him, and Armstrong plays masterly solos on two takes of the number and 'I'm Confessin''.

James C Petrillo (1892–1984), the son of a Chicago sewer man, rose through the city's musicians' union to become boss of the white branch, Local 10, and was elected president of the national federation in 1940. He feared no man, even sending a complaining cable to Mussolini after his consul in Chicago hired a non-union band, but he was pathologically afraid of infection, and refused to shake hands except by sticking out his little finger.

James C Petrillo

The Armed Forces got the first V-Discs in October 1943. They were 12-inch 78s with distinctive labels, carrying music of all kinds from all sources: reissues of commercial recordings and alternative takes, transcribed broadcasts, rehearsals and specially arranged sessions. The Armed Forces Radio Service also sent out 33rpm discs with a complete radio show on each side so that troops could hear them out of range of American transmitters. Performers, composers and the AFM waived fees and royalties; in return the services promised that all discs and masters would be destroyed after the war, so they would have no commercial value. In fact, servicemen often took them home and they were reissued, at first bootlegged and later permitted by unions and record companies when the war had been over for fifty years.

A second *Esquire* concert in January 1945 was actually three concerts, with portions of each broadcast nationally, ending with Duke Ellington's orchestra in Los Angeles accompanying solos by Benny Goodman in New York and Armstrong in New Orleans; to judge by a recording, neither of them could hear the accompaniment. Armstrong found himself leading a small band that included Sidney Bechet, whose competitive nature spurred him to try to take charge of the rehearsal. Armstrong's angry response, according to musicians who were there, was to yell: *I ain't gonna have no two leads in my band.*[148] On the recorded numbers, notably another magisterial 'I'm Confessin'', Bechet is unusually subdued. It seems they never met again.

Although Decca settled with the union before the other major labels, and the big band had gone into the studio as early as August 1944, Armstrong had grown keen enough on working with small groups for Leonard Feather, an English-born writer, composer and record-producer, to try to convince Joe Glaser that he would be better presented in a jazz context than as an entertainer fronting a big band. An opportunity came while Armstrong was appearing as an actor in the Hollywood film 'New Orleans' during the summer of 1946, and leading a small group as well as a big band on the soundtrack. Feather wanted Armstrong to make his debut at Carnegie Hall leading a small band but Armstrong resisted. Eventually they compromised: the evening, on 8 February 1947, ended with a big-band second half, but opened with Armstrong in front of the six-piece band which Edmond Hall, a New Orleans-born clarinet-player, was leading at a Greenwich Village nightclub.

Another promoter, Ernie Anderson, decided to try to prise Armstrong away from the big band, and believed that the idea would suit Glaser because of a chance encounter with him. One evening Anderson was strolling up 5th Avenue with a music-publisher friend, Lou Levy, when they spotted Glaser. Levy got Glaser to sign a document that listed Armstrong's compositions, and Anderson realised that the copyrights were being transferred to Levy's firm for $1,500. When Glaser had left, Levy admitted that he had a bargain, but said that Glaser needed cash urgently to pay the band's salaries, because it was short of bookings. Later Anderson found out that its fee had fallen to $350 for a weekday

Ernie Anderson (1910–95) was a hard-drinking ex-newspaperman who heard Armstrong in Paris in 1934 and became a fan. Back in New York, his hometown, he joined Eddie Condon, guitarist and saloon-keeper, to promote a series of concerts at Town Hall. After some years in London as a movie press agent, Anderson retired to Florida.

night or $600 for a Saturday. He got together with Bobby Hackett, a revered musician.

They drew up a list of tunes and musicians 'to present Armstrong playing with his peers in a programme of his classics'.[149] Armstrong was delighted with the idea, but said that Glaser would have to approve. Anderson got a certified cheque for $1,000 dollars made out to Glaser and took it to his office on 5th Avenue and 57th Street, where the waiting room was lined with performers, agents and managers hoping for a few words with the boss. Anderson handed the cheque to a telephone operator, who disappeared with it. Then, wrote Anderson later, 'the door out of the waiting room opened to reveal Joe, holding the check. He seemed to be in a purple rage. He threw a hostile glare at me and shouted, "What are you trying to do, you jerk?" I was deeply offended by this but I remained calm and said, "That's for Louis for one night without the band." After all I knew Joe Glaser well enough to know that he was never going to give up that check. Still snarling, he waved me through the

Bobby Hackett (1915–76) started out on ukelele and guitar, which gave him the harmonic knowledge to play unusual solos on cornet, including the beautifully oblique 12 bars on Glenn Miller's 'String of Pearls'. Fellow-musicians used to kid him about his inability to speak ill of anybody, except perhaps for the comedian Jackie Gleason, who hired him for a series of best-selling mood music albums that paid Hackett no royalties.

door and into his office.'[150] Tempted by Anderson's prediction that a new format for Armstrong would raise his nightly fee to $2,500, Glaser agreed that Louis would play a concert starting at 11.30 pm on Saturday, 17 May 1947, at Town Hall, a 1,500-seat auditorium on West 43rd Street, a block from Times Square.

Except for Armstrong's regular drummer, Sid Catlett, the band Hackett had rehearsed, playing Armstrong's parts himself, was white: it included Teagarden on trombone, Peanuts Hucko on clarinet and Dick Cary at the piano. Armstrong told the musicians he had no need to rehearse with them. Before a full house, he began the show accompanied by the rhythm section, dashing into 'Cornet Chop Suey' as if he were still the youngster who first recorded it 21 years before. The unrehearsed aspect of the concert became obvious when Cary tried to repeat 'My Monday Date' instead of starting 'Big Butter and Egg Man': Louis played along for half a chorus, then announced: *We're going to swing into 'Butter and Egg Man', folks.* The front line came on stage for 'Tiger Rag'; as the night went on the collaboration between Armstrong and Teagarden, and the warmth of Hackett's counter-melodies contrasting with Armstrong's brilliance, marked the concert as an artistic as well as financial triumph. Everyone was in a high good humour, and at the top of his form: on 'Back o' Town Blues', Armstrong laughingly silenced a heckler and lost track of the lyrics, so that he repeated the line *I must ask her to forgive me*, yet his timing was so exquisite that, without disturbing the rhythm, he was able to fit in the correct line, *It's going to bounce right back on you*. We know because Anderson had the foresight to have the concert recorded on wax discs, and RCA Victor, which at the time had Armstrong under contract, released three 12-inch 78s, picking out six tunes that would each fit on a side. They set a high standard, but the release of the rest of the show in the LP era revealed other masterpieces, including a storming 'St Louis Blues' and a joyful 'I Can't Give You Anything But Love'.

The Town Hall line-up: Teagarden, Cary, Armstrong, Hackett, Hucko, Bob Haggart and Catlett.

One person was missing: Sidney Bechet had been hired, but sent word that he was ill. Later people saw him working at his usual job in Jimmy Ryan's nightclub on 52nd Street. The next day Glaser, who had watching the concert from a box, gave the big band two weeks' notice, and signed Jack Teagarden to a seven-year contract, the maximum allowed by law. The All Stars were about to be born.

On Wednesday, 13 August 1947, Armstrong's new band played its first date. Ernie Anderson wanted to call it Louis Armstrong and His Concert Orchestra, but Joe Glaser insisted on billing it as Louis Armstrong and His All Stars – 'Joe makes it sound like a basketball team,' said Eddie Condon.[151] The choice of venue was paradoxical: Billy Berg's in Los Angeles, the club where Dizzy Gillespie

and Charlie Parker had brought their message of a new jazz, bop, to the West Coast in an historic residency at the end of 1945.

But there were advantages in going into the young lions' den, as the Californian saxophonist Sonny Criss recalled: 'Billy Berg's was a unique club, in the sense that it was in the centre of

Bop, or bebop, was evolved by young musicians rebelling against the heavily arranged big bands and established swing style: most boppers favoured small groups, unison theme statements and tunes based on the blues or popular songs but using a more complex harmonic language as the basis of extended improvisation. Rhythm sections, too, were more complex: the bass provided a steady pulse while the piano provided supporting chords for the soloist and the drummer played cross-rhythms in a development of Sid Catlett's approach. Soon jazz fans split into two warring parties: 'dirty boppers' *versus* 'mouldy fygges', as the boppers called traditionalists.

Hollywood, and it was the first really cosmopolitan club with a good deal of publicity behind it where negro and white people mixed without any pressure. It was a groovy atmosphere, an atmosphere that embraced people from all walks of life.'[152] As for publicity, Anderson, travelling with the band as an unpaid publicist, discovered that the club had been doing poor business, and Berg owed the *Los Angeles Times* so much that it refused to take any more advertising from him. Local disc-jockeys 'didn't seem too enthusiastic, so in desperation I sent out about a thousand telegrams to everybody in Hollywood listed by Celebrity Service. The telegrams worked and Bing Crosby led a show business invasion that packed the place out.'[153]

In spite of the success of the Berg's engagement, Anderson was sure that the All Stars' future was in the concert hall and Glaser let him have Armstrong for dates at Carnegie Hall in New York and Symphony Hall in Boston. Anderson took a tape recorder, one of the first available, to Carnegie Hall and was playing the tape to guests at an after-show party when Armstrong arrived and was amazed to realise he was listening to the concert he had just performed. Next day he bought himself two machines. Anderson had the Boston concert professionally recorded, and it was eventually issued on a pair of LPs, the earliest of a series of All Stars concerts to appear in that way. Four of the men who played at Town Hall – Armstrong, Catlett, Teagarden and Cary – had now been joined by the clarinet-player Barney Bigard and the bass-player Arvell Shaw.

The ensemble was completed by Velma Middleton, a mountainous woman whose speciality was rattling stages to their foundations by doing the splits. 'No doubt about it the audience was always shaken and generally impressed. Getting up posed a problem. She solved it by considering her act over when she hit the floor, and scrambled to her feet after the spotlight died.'[154] Her purpose in the group was to act as a comedy stooge for Armstrong and sing, with him or by herself. Her singing was not good: the records suggest that she found it hard to hit a note except by scooping up to it from below, and hard to hold on to it once she had hit it. Promoters and record-producers tried to keep her off stage, but Armstrong always insisted on her presence, and other members of the All Stars recognised her achievements. 'They were a fantastic team together,' said the trombonist Trummy Young. 'Velma wasn't a great singer or nothing like that, but she certainly was the right foil for Louis. I would have hated to follow them two on stage, man.'[155] And Jack Lesberg, who later played bass in the group, said: 'She was funny and he'd get a kick out of her, she was so big and fat. He knew the people liked it as entertainment. He was electric on that stage.'[156]

In contrast Dick Cary was an accomplished pianist, brass-player and arranger, but no showman. After a couple of years with the All Stars he left, saying he was bored, and that made room for Earl Hines, who had showmanship in plenty. The change justified the All Star title: even young Shaw, in the supporting role, was pleasing the public with his featured solo on 'How High the Moon', sneaking in some bop phrases. But for all their long acquaintance, Hines was not Louis's closest musical partner in the band. That distinction belonged to Jack Teagarden.

Barney Bigard (1906–80) brought New Orleans clarinet into Duke Ellington's band from 1927 to 1940. The last of three stints with the All Stars ended in 1961, when he went into semi-retirement in California. 'He always played the Albert system, and he had that woody tone which I love on the instrument,' wrote Ellington. 'He was invaluable for putting the filigree work into an arrangement.'[157]

Arvell Shaw (1923–2002) joined Armstrong's big band in St Louis in 1945, moving on to the All Stars at a time when only a couple of bass-players could remotely be called stars. Armstrong gave him solos and Shaw developed as a showman, a smiling bear-like presence looming over the big instrument and setting a rock-steady pulse. He worked on and off with Armstrong until Louis's last engagement.

Armstrong and Teagarden had a personal and musical rapport which made their collaborations like informal conversations between friends, whether they were playing, singing or joking around on 'Rockin' Chair'. They appeared together on television with Eddie Condon – another Ernie Anderson venture – and when tours took them to the West Coast, on radio with Bing Crosby. In 1950s America Teagarden's presence in what was therefore a

Jack Teagarden (1905–64) came from a musical family in Vernon, Texas, and astounded New York musicians when he got there in 1927 by his instrumental facility, his tone, his ideas and his blues-based singing. His extraordinary lip control meant that he rarely had to move the trombone slide beyond the three positions nearest to the mouthpiece. Jack's first instrument had been a peck horn, with valves, and his brother Charlie, a fine trumpeter, said it stuck with him: 'Jack never thought of his trombone as a slide instrument.'[158] As for his singing, the critic Whitney Balliett wrote: 'The rare consonants he used sounded like vowels, and his vowels were all puréed. His vocals were lullabies – lay-me-down-to-sleep patches of sound.'[159] Drink, debt and alimony drove Teagarden to join Paul Whiteman's dance band for five years in the 30s: then he took his own swing band on the road, and was soon $46,000 in debt. He spent four years with the All Stars.

I think Jack Teagarden moves me more than any musician I know of, right through here.[160]

'mixed' band could have made difficulties in the South, but Armstrong insisted that his tours there were *wonderful, everywhere but Memphis. I couldn't have Jack on the stand there, so we don't play there at all. Down in Houston, Texas, they have separate sections for coloured and white. But when we play there they all come down to the bandstand together, and there's nobody looking around to see who's behind them; they don't care. We notice all that.*[161]

In the battle that was splitting the jazz world in two, the All Stars were perceived by some as being on the side of the revivalists, because of Louis's presence as a representative of the New Orleans tradition and the trumpet-trombone-clarinet front line; certainly Armstrong had harsh things to say against the boppers, condemning *modern slop*[162] and *weird chords which don't mean nothing.*[163] But the self-appointed guardians of the sacred torch of purism had written off everything after 'Potato Head Blues' in 1927 as a betrayal: the arch-purist Rudi Blesh described 'West End Blues' as 'a record of great beauty although it narrowly misses banality' and condemned it for 'departing from the jazz concept'.[164] Reviled by both factions for playing swing, Louis, to the delight of the non-specialists and the general public, went on leading the finest small swing band of all time. He allowed his soloists plenty of time in the spotlight, but was watchful of abuse that might damage the performance. At the 1948 jazz festival in Nice, Humphrey Lyttelton, now the doyen of British jazzmen, then a young trumpeter and fan, met him and sent home a telegram: 'Have shaken hands with Louis Armstrong.'[165] Standing behind the bandstand one night he was awed by Armstrong's command over his gathering of giants: 'I found myself quaking at the ferocity with which he directed the band. If Sid Catlett's drums started to intrude too heavily upon a solo, Louis would turn and hiss at him like a snake. And more than once Earl Hines's exuberance was curbed by a sharp: *Cut it, boy!*'[166] Arvell Shaw saw another side of his methods: 'Some bandleaders I've known and worked for, when you had a solo and you got a real big hand, you didn't get another solo. I worked with one: I won't call names, but he played clarinet. Everybody in the All Stars got a chance, your spot where you went out and did your thing, your solo spot. He wanted you to go out there and get a standing ovation if you could, stand on your eyelashes and get a standing ovation – he loved that. Because he knew that all he had to do was walk right up behind you, smile, unfurl that handkerchief and look at the audience and he'd wash you away! And it wasn't an ego thing, it was just the way it was. Because he realised the better you were the better it made his band.'[167]

Glaser set a relentless pace of touring, but Armstrong objected if he had days off, because he needed to play often to keep his lip in shape. *Oh, Pops. If I take a vacation, my lips will go down,*[168] he used to say. Although they were well paid, the rigours of the road were punishing, and the mighty All Stars began to break up in 1949. Big Sid Catlett, for all his power, had an enlarged heart after a childhood bout of rheumatic fever: his first heart attack came after a night's work at Billy Berg's in Hollywood, and he left the band in Chicago soon after. Glaser sent him to the mountains for a rest, but rest was not in his character. Shaw said: 'He loved life. He loved to play cards. He loved to gamble. He loved women. He liked to be around the guys. He didn't like to waste his time sleeping.'[169] Catlett died in 1951. His All Star replacement was Cozy Cole, a fine drummer whose rhythm nevertheless did not stand comparison with Sid's.

The same year Hines and Teagarden both quit. Teagarden had actually announced his intention to leave in the summer of 1949, but Glaser, who held his contract, probably made it impossible for him to go. Hines, formerly a successful bandleader in his own right, had a dispute over billing. 'I had had a contract with 75 per cent publicity and a good salary, but they wanted to list me merely as a sideman. I though they should have kept me with 75 per cent publicity, but they were not going to, so that was my reason for leaving.'[170] Asked how he felt about losing Hines, Armstrong reacted angrily. *I don't give a damn. Hines and his ego, ego, ego! If he wanted to go, the hell with him. He's good, sure, but we don't need him,* he told a reporter. *Earl Hines and his big ideas. Well, we can get along without Mr Earl Hines.* But he added: *What really bothers me, Pops, is losing Jack. That Teagarden, man, he's like my brother. We've worked together so fine these last few years.* His theory was that Teagarden's wife wanted him to stay at home in Texas. *Pops won't make any money that way, away from us. I don't think Jack really wanted to leave. It isn't like him to do that. Sometimes people don't do the things they really want to do.*[171]

Hines led a series of small bands, eventually basing himself in San Francisco, and his career faded until three concerts in New York in 1964 earned him a comeback. His former sidemen were fond of him, but there was no doubt about his personal vanity: as he grew balder he wore a toupee that made him look as though a stuffed bird had been attached to his head, and at the 1974 Nice festival he insisted on staying at the splendid and expensive Negresco, instead of the modest hotel where the other musicians were living. But after two days he relented and came to join the after-hours talk and music, leaving the toupee behind.

Jack Teagarden also led small bands, with reasonable success, but in a subdued way: 'You couldn't hear him from two feet away,' the trombonist Chris Barber remembered.[172] The clarinet-player Kenny Davern, who worked for him, believes that Teagarden's 'ego was all shot down' and he was suffering from depression, although he had stopped drinking. 'He took care of business, but it was like because he had to. I didn't think maybe he even wanted to be there,' says Davern. At home Teagarden worked at a lathe, making mouthpieces 'by the hog-barrel-full.

On the road, he used to smoke a joint and tune the piano. He tuned the piano every day in the period I was with him.' Later Davern was playing at the Metropole, a midtown Manhattan bar, when Teagarden walked in with his fourth wife, Addie. 'When I came off the bandstand to say hello, he said: "I don't know if you remember me, Kenny . . . I'm Jack Teagarden." '[173]

King of the Zulus

Most of the men who played at Town Hall turned up again a month later on the stage of the Winter Garden Theater in New York to play an hour-long broadcast concert as part of the premiere of 'New Orleans', a feature film 'which traces the history of jazz from Basin Street to Carnegie Hall', as the NBC radio announcer put it. The screenplay had undergone drastic revision under the looming threat of the witch-hunt for Communist sympathisers in Hollywood, so the races were once again segregated and Woody Herman's white big band wound up playing in the concert hall, while Armstrong's band played in the street. As his bass-player in the movie, Red Callender, recalled: 'As great a singer as Billie Holiday was, her part was just a maid. Armstrong was some sort of handyman who happened to play trumpet.'[174] Although the picture was quickly forgotten, it included a new song, 'Do You Know What It Means to Miss New Orleans?': sung by Holiday on the screen, it was instantly appropriated by Armstrong for his stage repertoire. United Artists' publicity for the movie also raised Louis's profile among the general public: he began to make frequent appearances on radio and TV shows, particularly with Bing Crosby – Armstrong and Crosby fitted neatly together as singers, producing a hit record with 'Gone Fishin''.

Armstrong also got more movie roles, mostly as himself – in 'The Glenn Miller Story' with James Stewart, 'The Five Pennies', a biopic of the cornetist Red Nichols, played by Danny Kaye, and most successfully of all in 'High Society', for which he joined Crosby, Frank Sinatra and Grace Kelly in a musical remake of 'The Philadelphia Story' moved from the Main Line in

Armstrong and Grace Kelly on the set of 'High Society'

Philadelphia to another patrician neighbourhood, Newport, Rhode Island, which just happened to be staging an annual jazz festival. Cole Porter's score lets Armstrong, Crosby and the All Stars bounce their way through 'Now You Has Jazz'. Armstrong introduces the film and gives an exposition of the plot in 'High Society Calypso', a device imitating the opening of Bertholt Brecht and Kurt Weill's 'Threepenny Opera' when the Street Singer performs 'The Ballad of Mack the Knife' – a big hit for Armstrong the year before in 1954.

Before making 'New Orleans' Louis had returned to his home town for a visit that coincided with Mardi Gras. He and Lucille were carried round the celebrating city on the float of the Zulu Social Aid and Pleasure Club, an African-American burial society, along with the King of Zulus, a member of the club which aimed to make fun of the white 'krewes' whose floats dominate the parade.

At Mardi Gras in 1949 he took on the role himself, in blackface make-up with white circles around his eyes and mouth, and dressed in a grass skirt, a wig and a feathered crown. Throughout the day his float took him on an eccentric route through the crowds so that he could throw 20,000 coconuts at them. Some of Armstrong's fans thought the costume undignified and Dizzy Gillespie denounced him as a 'plantation character'.[176]

In spite of their close working relationship, Louis suspected Bing Crosby of racism. The bassist Jack Lesberg said that Louis 'just felt that he'd never been to his home. This bothered him very much. Bing just didn't realise how sensitive a man Louis was.'[175]

Louis took it as an honour. He wrote to a fan: *The Zulus Social Aid and Pleasure Club was originated in the neighbourhood that I was reared . . . all the members of the Zulus are people for generations most of them brought up right there around Perdido and Franklin Streets . . . So finally I grew into manhood – ahem – and the life-long ambition never did cease.*[177]

He recalled as he was being made up by a Zulu member that his stepfather – he did not say which one – had worn the same blackface, and he later described Willie Armstrong's love of parades: *My real dad was a sharp man, tall and handsome and well built. He made the chicks swoon when he marched by as the grandmarshal in the Odd Fellows parade. I was very proud to see him in his uniform and his high hat with the beautiful streamer hanging down by his side. Yes, he was a fine figure of a man, my dad.*[178] The past came back to him when he and the All Stars played a show in the evening; a woman claiming to be Mrs Louis Armstrong insisted

I have travelled all over the world and no place that I've ever been could remove the thought that was in my head – that some day I will be King of the Zulus[179]

on being admitted free, and turned out to be Daisy, his knife-wielding first wife. Armstrong's sister, Mama Lucy lived in New Orleans until her death on 12 January 1987.

Armstrong was keen to set down his life story in a better way than *Swing That Music*, and recruited the Belgian critic Robert Goffin, who had fled the war in Europe, as ghost-writer, sending him anecdotes and details of his youth, as well as cash to support him in America. *Horn of Plenty* appeared in 1947, but it was quickly clear that Goffin had made a mess of the job, partly because of his inadequate English and the bizarre version of New Orleans black speech that he used for invented dialogue. Armstrong's hopes of a movie based on the book, which he had discussed with Orson Welles on one of his Hollywood visits, vanished.

So he went to work by himself, and wrote – single-space typing on his favourite yellow paper – hundreds of pages about his childhood and youth. A French translation appeared in 1952, and the English-language version two years later. *Satchmo: My Life in New Orleans* had been tidied up by an editor, but it was recognisably Armstrong's own work in essence. The book was acclaimed, and Armstrong started on a sequel about his discovery of marijuana and his time as a young musician in the Chicago of speakeasies and gangsters, the sort of people Joe Glaser hung out with. He showed what he had written to Glaser, who carefully destroyed it. Armstrong went on writing his story for the rest of his life, and much detail also emerges in his letters to friends and fans.

In 1956 the Decca Record Co. came up with another project for him. They put him in a studio with his current group of All Stars, together with some other fine musicians and a brace of brilliant arrangers, and asked him to play three hours or so of jazz to create a box set called 'Satchmo: A Musical Autobiography'. The sessions were an important indication of Armstrong's status as an artist and entertainer; the label had produced two years earlier a similarly grand musical autobiography for its other big talent, Bing Crosby, also a genuine star on a global scale. Milt Gabler, the producer who looked after Armstrong's recordings for Decca and had started the independent Commodore jazz label before the war, persuaded Glaser to take the All Stars off the road temporarily, so that they could make recordings without having to go on to perform in public the same day, and to add a concert payment to their session fee. That may be why the Autobiography sessions sound so relaxed and happy.

The All Stars by that time had settled down after a period of upheaval: the trombone was Trummy Young, the clarinet Ed Hall, and the pianist Billy Kyle. Squire Gersh played the bass, and the drummer was Barrett Deems. Louis introduces the set, speaking quietly over some subtle piano by Billy Kyle, who quotes the Armstrong theme song, 'When It's Sleepy Time Down South'. These little speeches between tracks are one of the delights of the set; they remind us not only of Louis's unique voice but also of his astounding talent for achieving instant intimacy with an audience, whether it was 30,000 in a football stadium or a lone listener beside a loudspeaker. The words, however, are not his, and he sometimes sounds awkward reading them. They were written by Leonard Feather, who occasionally walks a tightrope of imprecision, while only once falling into a downright untruth or error. Armstrong tells us: *I want to bring back the music just the way it was played in those good ol' days*, but that is not exactly what happens. The King Oliver numbers diverge a long way from the tradition of collective improvisation which the original versions represent, emphasising solos instead, in the style we now call mainstream. The arranger, Bob Haggart, brought in his long-time partner Yank Lawson to play lead trumpet, leaving Louis, as in 1923, with the second part. Armstrong, though, takes Oliver's solo on 'Dippermouth Blues', using an open instead of a muted horn as if to avoid comparison with his old boss. Trummy Young seems to make an effort on these reconstructions of early sides at a primitive, rasping sound and a wild and woolly execution which is not entirely successful, though he cleans his act

Billy Kyle (1914–66) built an unusual and witty single-note style on a foundation of Earl Hines. He found a natural home with John Kirby in 'The Biggest Little Band in the Land', which broke up after he was drafted into the army. Armstrong plucked him out of Broadway pit bands, including two years in 'Guys and Dolls'.

Barrett Deems (1913–98) had a formidable drumming technique and wrote a practice manual. His career was based in Chicago, where he led bands through the 30s before joining the great violinist Joe Venuti from 1938 to 1944. Deems returned to Chicago and freelancing after the All Stars, touring with Goodman and the Dukes of Dixieland.

up for later periods. Ed Hall, the clarinetist from New Orleans, sticks to his own swing-era style; he fudges the famous Alphonse Picou solo in 'High Society', but so did Johnny Dodds on the original. 'Nobody played it note for note,' Ed was once reported to have declared: Pee Wee Russell refused to play it at all.

For Billy Kyle the Autobiography is a triumph; the vigour of his solos is balanced by the sensitivity of his interludes accompanying Louis's narrative. Armstrong recalls having recorded, 'Of All The Wrongs You've Done To Me', with Clarence Williams, in November 1924 as a moonlighting member of the Fletcher Henderson orchestra in New York. He also recorded it two days earlier with Alberta Hunter and the Red Onion Jazz Babies, another studio band, and the arrangement for the Autobiography version owes more to that recording. 'Everybody Loves My Baby' was also recorded by both groups: Louis doesn't mention the Williams version, perhaps because his solo was shoved out of the way by a swaggering soprano saxophone: people are still arguing about whether it is Bechet or Buster Bailey acting under Bechet's influence. Louis talks of his association with Bechet before playing 'Mandy Make Up Your Mind', in which we get a first solo from the guitarist George Barnes, added to these recordings of early pieces which used a guitar or banjo in the rhythm section: rhythm guitars were out of fashion by 1956. Barnes was an irascible virtuoso who in

Edmond Hall (1901–67) was a New Orleans player with a sharp, cutting sound on his Albert system clarinet, although he picked up some of Benny Goodman's phrases. After working in Claude Hopkins's big band and leading some beautiful small group recordings with the guitarist Charlie Christian, he joined Eddie Condon's house band, then Louis.

Trummy Young (1912–84) was a major trombone soloist in Earl Hines's big band and became a star with Jimmie Lunceford's, singing in a confidential breathy style on 'Margie' and other hits. But he also recorded some early bop with Parker and Gillespie. He married a girl from Hawaii and worked there until recruited by Armstrong.

the 70s co-led a brilliant but strife-torn quartet with the cornetist Ruby Braff. On 'Mandy' he sounds oddly countrified, but his later contributions exploit his blues-based style effectively.

The low point of the set calls on Velma Middleton to take the roles of four of the great blues singers of the 1920s. Velma, for all her size, was a lightweight singer. In 'Reckless Blues', given Bessie Smith's line, 'Momma wants some lovin' right now', Velma sounds as if she is perched on a stool at a brightly lit soda-fountain; Bessie sounds as if she is sprawled on a big brass bed beside a dimly glowing oil lamp. 'Georgia Grind', a few numbers later, is more Velma's material, giving her a chance for smiling showbiz singing, with a beautiful obbligato contributed by Ed Hall. Two tracks made by previous editions of the All Stars with Cozy Cole or Sid Catlett on drums make it all the more sad that Louis's regular drummer at the time of the Autobiography sessions was Barrett Deems. His stiff, unyielding beat, as insensitive as a hippo's hide and made obvious by a close recording, casts a blight on the whole project. Deems's status as an All Star was based on his billing as 'the world's fastest drummer'. Oddly, on records away from the band he can sound much less rigid, though still emphatic. Arvell Shaw said: 'Barrett was a good solid drummer and dependable. We made some good recordings with him – the best one was WC Handy. Louis liked Barrett's playing. It was steady. It wasn't New Orleans-type drumming, but the All Stars was not a New Orleans type of band.'[180] Even Deems contributes to the 1956–7 All Stars' storming version of the Hot Five number 'King of the Zulus', a threatening minor-key blues. Louis's first formidable solo is interrupted by Trummy Young, putting on a Jamaican accent which isn't good enough to fool Armstrong, who calls him *Geechie* - a term for people from Georgia, the state where he was born. Young's solo is splendid, full of his own character, and it leads up to another magnificent contribution from Armstrong.

There are four blues-based numbers in which Armstrong was originally partnered by Johnny Dodds's forceful clarinet, either in the Hot Seven or under Dodds's leadership. Hall, for all the occasional rough edge on his tone, was a more polite player than Dodds, and Armstrong seems to take over Dodds's role with a series of dramatic solos – grim, even, on 'Wild Man Blues' – which are nonetheless played with very beautiful tone, particularly lovely in the little tag which ends 'Gully Low'. On the Hot Five 'Struttin' with Some Barbecue' Armstrong phrases very freely, spurred on, as so often, by the use of stop time; the performance is carefully thought out and witty. The Autobiography version, from a live concert, has a smooth solo and a Dixieland ending, conventional compared to the original. But for sheer beauty of tone neither can touch the 1938 version with big band. 'Two Deuces' heralds a new era of the Hot Five, with Earl Hines instead of the slapdash Lil Hardin on piano. It gives Billy Kyle a chance to imitate his hero, down to an odd, atmospheric tremolo passage. And it raises the question of the missing records, the ones which Armstrong did not re-record for the Autobiography. The exclusion of 'Weather Bird', his classic duet with Hines, could be due to the bad feeling between the two when Hines left the All Stars. Certainly Armstrong seems to have re-written history for the Autobiography, claiming on the last disc that 'Dear Old Southland', first made with Buck Washington at the keyboard more than a year after 'Weather Bird', was *the first trumpet solo I ever recorded with just a piano*. Armstrong may have forgotten that the main reason for making 'Dear Old Southland' was to provide a suitable coupling for the delayed release of 'Weather Bird'. But it seems more likely that he wanted to take a swipe at Hines. Another glaring omission is less easily explained. 'West End Blues' is not even mentioned in the Autobiography.

The 1957 version of 'Knockin' a Jug' gives Young a chance to express his admiration for Teagarden without actually imitating him, and Barnes, while different in approach to Eddie Lang, has the right bluesy style. There is also some nice tenor sax from Seldon Powell, one of the extra reeds brought in by Sy Oliver, the former arranger for Jimmie Lunceford and Tommy Dorsey, who had charge of the bands for most of the rest of the Autobiography. Armstrong's own contribution includes a different cadenza; more thoughtful, less spontaneous, but elegantly phrased. Oliver's strategy with all his work on the Autobiography was clearly to examine the original big-band arrangements and meticulously throw them away, replacing them with updated charts, often based on the Dixieland-style ensembles which had proved so successful with Dorsey's band-within-a-band, the Clambake Seven. This was almost twenty years before the wave of stylish re-creations of past jazz arrangements by Bob Wilber, Dick Hyman and others with the New York Jazz Repertory Company and by Alan Cohen and Brian Priestley, for example, in Britain.

Before 'I Can't Give You Anything But Love' Armstrong tells us, *I guess this was my first time singing a popular hit song.* The songs that make up most of the rest of the Autobiography were in Armstrong's repertoire for longer than the instrumental pieces, and he naturally felt more relaxed with them. Occasionally that made him fall into a routine performance, but that does not seem to happen in the Autobiography, perhaps because of the unusual circumstances and the new arrangements. The collection comes to a splendid end with a particularly fiery finale to 'On the Sunny Side of the Street', which he first recorded, in front of the barely-competent pick-up band in Paris, during October 1934. And that, to judge from the Autobiography, is when Louis Armstrong's career stopped. There are no re-creations after that date; Armstrong thanks his colleagues and bids us all a throaty farewell.

Did he decide not to re-record 'Swing That Music' or 'West End Blues', which he had remade in 1939, because he thought he might not be up to it, that his lip might give way? Certainly there are moments in the Autobiography when he seems to duck away from the high notes. But the more likely reason is that 'Swing That Music', the 1939 'West End Blues' and a hundred or more other sides were recorded for Decca. Only a handful of tunes already recorded by Decca was remade for the Autobiography; odd as it now appears, it looks as though Decca wanted the Autobiography to cover recordings made by other companies, and not to go out of its way to compete with existing Decca records which might still have some commercial life left in them – although Decca was simply reissuing a few of them in haphazard LP compilations. Whatever the reason, and however much we might regret not hearing Armstrong's later thoughts on 'West End Blues', we can be grateful for the remarkable insight into his music that the Autobiography gives us, not least because it drives us back to the original records and makes them sound fresh.

The gruelling schedule of national and international tours which Glaser set for the All Stars lasted for almost a quarter of a century: it is a remarkable feat for a band with a largely stable personnel and a restricted repertoire. Or, to put it another way, it was difficult to understand how the same group of musicians could play the same material in the same way night after night. Armstrong invariably started his shows with 'Sleepy Time Down South', coming downstage with arms extended and the same greeting to the audience: *Good evenin' everybody!* The next number would be 'Indiana', the next 'Blueberry Hill' and the concert would unroll steadily through *the good ol' good ones*, interrupted by any Armstrong record that happened to be a current hit. While the general public whistled and stamped at the first notes of 'Mack the Knife' or 'Hello, Dolly', to jazz fans Louis and the All Stars seemed to have fossilised. Record-producers saw little point in new concert recordings of the same tunes, and brought Louis into the studio with unusual material, such as a magnificent album of W C Handy compositions, only one of which, 'St Louis Blues', was part of Armstrong's usual repertoire.

Joe Muranyi, born in Ohio in 1928, studied with the modernist guru Lennie Tristano, but worked in Dixieland bands with leaders such as Bobby Hackett and Eddie Condon, and led his own Village Stompers before joining the All Stars in 1967. After Armstrong's death he joined Roy Eldridge's band at Jimmy Ryan's in New York. Now a freelance, Muranyi also produces records and is writing his own book about Armstrong.

'The whole Handy album, I don't think he played any of those things after he recorded it,' Trummy Young said. 'We had a big repertoire, but he just stuck with things he felt had won over audiences for him . . . he stuck with those all the time. He could get away with it because we were travelling all the time. It was amazing how we could get the proper feel of those tunes every night, because that's hard to do without going stale.'[181]

Joe Muranyi, Armstrong's last clarinet-player, explained what could happen if a programme changed: 'The programmes were sort of the same, but Armstrong kept himself fresh on his complete repertoire. I think he could play anything he'd recorded, and sometimes somebody would be very insistent on a request and he'd play it, and the band would be stumped.'[182]

The All Stars had no physical 'book' of parts to read on stage. They memorised any arrangements, particularly of the new material which Armstrong might record as a pop record with such arrangers as Sy Oliver and Gordon Jenkins. 'When they figured that something was going to be a hit, we'd put it in the repertoire. In the studio it could be quite written, and then you'd memorise,' said Muranyi. 'Like "Blueberry Hill": in the middle there's a unison with the trombone and clarinet which is from the original Gordon Jenkins record. It just became part of the thing – it sounded as if it were improvised, but it was actually written.' Joe Darensbourg held the clarinet spot in 1963 when the All Stars recorded 'Hello Dolly', using a Billy Kyle arrangement; it began to climb the charts while they were in Puerto Rico: 'Louis says: *Any of you guys remember this damn tune?* Billy could only remember some parts, so we had to run all round San Juan trying to find the single. Couldn't find it, so they had to fly one out of New York to us and we listened to it . . . and the very first time Louis did it on stage in Hotel San Juan he had to take about eight curtain calls, so he knew right then he had a hit.'[183]

Armstrong himself was accused of repeating his solos note for note. But Muranyi said: 'Louis Armstrong was a composer, really, when he played. He had a very good musical mind and he arranged things – he had outlines for his solos: when we hear Louis we know right away it's Louis because there are certain things he does; it's always identifiable on account of that, but it doesn't make him any less wonderful. He created them, and so the outline would often be the same, but the details would be different.'[184] Jack Lesberg said the performance 'didn't change much except that it was very spontaneous, extremely spontaneous'. Glaser would want Armstrong to change the programme because he read criticism of it, but *What the hell*, Armstrong said, *Nobody plays it the way I play it. These are my songs the way I play them.*[185]

Glaser had, however, a say in the choice of personnel, and sometimes moved in mysterious ways. There was a crisis when Hines was replaced by Joe Sullivan, and Armstrong found him unsatisfactory – it may have been the almost inevitable distaste of a pot-smoker for a heavy drinker. He was fired, and Glaser hired Marty Napoleon, a swing pianist, simply because he had worked briefly in his uncle Phil Napoleon's Dixieland band. Quitting could be problematical. Trummy Young told Kenny Davern that he found it impossible to leave the All Stars until the moment they were about to fly out on a South American tour. At the airport he hung back when they neared the gate and took a flight home to Hawaii instead. Davern said: 'He kept saying to Glaser, "Look, I've got to leave, I'm tired, I've been on the band a long time," and Glaser kept yessing him, saying, "We're looking for a replacement for you, can you hang around a little longer?" That went on for a year or two and Trummy finally said, "The hell with this", and went to Hawaii, and then they had to get a replacement.'[186] Barrett Deems got fired by Glaser, says the trombonist and writer Jim Beebe, 'although Louis loved Barrett and wanted him on the band. Deems had become a pariah with his prickly personality and had caused scenes throughout Europe. Deems told me that Glaser made it very difficult for him if he wanted to stay with the band. He was never honest about getting fired – for years he maintained that he quit.'[187]

On tour, absences had to be covered by musicians from the local union membership. When Jack Teagarden had a night's ill-

Russ Phillips on tour with the All Stars

ness in Denver, Colorado, the trombonist Russ Phillips was planning to join the audience and found himself playing instead. He told his son, also named Russ, that after Teagarden resigned Armstrong asked Barney Bigard and Cozy Cole who they would like in the band. 'They said: "Get the fat white cat from Denver!" Those were their very words,' said the son.[188] Phillips, who had been playing in the pit band of the Chicago Theater, a 4,300-seat variety palace – and was a fine musician, to judge by his obbligato behind Armstrong on his recording of 'I'll Walk Alone' – had moved to Denver when he got married and had a child. At the age of four, Russ the younger found himself on the road with the Armstrong All Stars and his mother Jocelyn.

'My mom and I went everywhere with him, all over the country – wherever the band went, that's where we were: we rode on the bus, or the airplane or whatever mode of transport,' he said. 'Barney's wife, Dorthe, and Cozy's wife at the time, and Velma were like a family to me. Even as a child I remember how gracious Louis was.' His parents had pictures of the band working in halls that were 'not like the venues where you'd think that somebody of Louis's stature should be playing. Part of that was the black–white situation at the time. Some of the places were brutal.'[189] When Russ reached school age the band would be obliged to hire a tutor for him, so the Phillips family settled back in Chicago, where he now plays trombone. His father was replaced by Trummy Young, who had sat in when Armstrong visited Hawaii: 'They hit it off so well, musically, that Louis wanted him on the band,' said Jim Beebe.[190] Kenny Davern was offered the clarinet job in 1967, and described how two of Glaser's men made him roll up his sleeves because 'we don't want junkies with the star.' They offered $500 a week, with $50 raises every six months, and he was considering the offer when one of them phoned to ask his suit size and tell him to start with the band in four days' time. When Davern pointed out that he had several months' bookings to fulfil, the caller snarled 'Good luck to you,' and hung up.[191]

The bass player Joe Levinson described how he was asked to audition as a replacement for Arvell Shaw, who did not want to go on a Far East tour. He met Billy Kyle and drummer Danny Barcelona in a Manhattan studio and they started to play together. 'After a number or two I began to get the distinct impression that someone was seated in the shadows, way back of me. I looked and saw Satch sitting there, head bowed a little, almost as though he was sleeping, but I knew he wasn't. He didn't come forward. He didn't say a word.' Ten minutes later, Kyle stopped the audition and told Levinson he would hear the result. He packed and left. 'Satch never got up, never said a word.'[192] Levinson was surprised when he was offered the job: but in the end Shaw decided to go on the tour.

Shaw added up the numbers of people on the road: 'There'd be the band. That's six pieces. Then the singer, that's seven, then the band valet, then Louis had his personal valet, that's nine, then the road manager, then the doctor sometimes, later on after he had his heart attack, would travel with us, then the guys who looked after the staging, so there were about fourteen or fifteen. When we were doing one-nighters, we had a very large bus for the fifteen. Other than that we would fly or take the train – all first class. At that time it was the highest-paid band. If you work together night after night for all the years, some nights you come in and you forget to speak: it becomes more like a family than a band. But it was a good job in the best conditions you could possibly find.'[193]

Shaw had taken the job in the original All Stars which Jack Lesberg had turned down because he was offered only $150 a week. Lesberg estimated that Teagarden and Catlett were on about $800 each in 1947. He said that when he toured with Armstrong later, 'Everything was laid on for comfort.

Each member of the band had five suits and one was always ready and pressed for you to wear in plenty of time before you went on. There was always a car to take you to wherever you had to play, and the same to take you back to your hotel. A meal was always ready at whatever time.'[194] And until Armstrong became

'He was a saint. He was the softest touch in the world. Whenever I went in to his dressing room . . . it would be full of broken-down musicians and show-biz types looking for a buck. It finally got so that Joe Glaser, who managed Pops most of his life, put a twenty-dollar lid on each handout. Even so, he helped support hundreds of people. It was one of his greatest pleasures.'

–Bobby Hackett[195]

ill late in life, there were no long layoffs, said Muranyi: 'He loved working: that was his life, playing his horn. He was accustomed to the road, the road was his home.'[196]

His dressing room was where he met friends and fans, often wearing nothing but a handkerchief tied round his head and a pair of underpants, handing out tins of lip salve made in Mannheim, packets of Swiss Kriss herbal laxative from Milwaukee with the message to 'Leave it all behind ya', 20 dollar bills and even Chrysler Imperial sedans. At London's Empress Hall in 1956, Humphrey Lyttelton saw him buttonholed by a notorious bore. 'Lucille was heard to murmur, "That guy's boring Louis to death!" and some friends offered to go in and rescue him. "Oh, don't do that," she begged earnestly, "If Louis thinks you don't like the guy, he'll feel sorry for him and talk to him all night!"'[197] Arvell Shaw said: 'He really did not have any idea of his own greatness. His mind didn't work that way. He was a very warm, kind human being, you know, he could talk to kings, presidents, popes, and he could talk to the ordinary man on the street – to him they were all people. That's the way he was. He was like most truly great men: he was a simple man.'[198] And Barney Bigard said: 'Louis was exactly the same on stage as off stage. Exactly. There never was any hidden side to him. You bought what you saw with him. He came "as is" . . . Now if somebody provoked him, that was a different thing. You'd get the greatest cussing out you ever heard, but he would have to be at the absolute end of his patience before he would ever be that way.'[199]

Black and Blue

The President of the United States and the Governor of Arkansas provoked Louis Armstrong one day in September 1957. Armstrong, due to play a concert in Grand Forks, North Dakota, settled down in his dressing room to watch the televison news before being interviewed for the local small-town newspaper. By the time the reporter arrived, Armstrong was furious. He had seen film of white supremacists in Arkansas yelling and spitting at a group of black children and their parents who were trying to enter school, and he announced he was withdrawing from a State Department-sponsored visit to the Soviet Union because *the way they are treating my people in the South, the Government can go to hell.*[200]

In failing to enforce the Supreme Court judgment outlawing school segregation, Armstrong said, President Eisenhower *may have no guts* – perhaps a reference to Eisenhower's colostomy in June 1956 – *but he has two faces*. As for Governor Faubus, *he's just a fool and an uneducated ploughboy*. The reporter showed his notes to Armstrong, who signed them and added: *Solid*. Next morning his road-man-

The United States Supreme Court delivered its unanimous judgment in the case of Brown v. Board of Education of Topeka on 17 May 1954, declaring that the practice of 'separate but equal' education for blacks and whites was unconstitutional. The father of Linda Brown, a ten-year-old when the case started, was the first on the list of plaintiffs backed by the National Association for the Advancement of Colored People. White resistance made progress to desegregation slow, and in September 1957 Governor Orval Faubus of Arkansas called in the National Guard to prevent black children from attending Central High School at Little Rock, the state capital.

ager, Pierre Tallerie, known as Frenchy, told reporters Armstrong 'was sorry he spouted off'. Louis woke up, fired Frenchy, and told the press: *Do you dig me when I still say I have a right to blow my top over injustice?*[201] On 24 September, after Eisenhower at last decided to back the Supreme Court by ordering 1,200 paratroopers to Little Rock, Louis sent him a congratulatory wire: *MR PRESIDENT. DADDY IF AND WHEN YOU DECIDE TO TAKE THOSE LITTLE NEGRO CHILDREN PERSONALLY INTO CENTRAL HIGH SCHOOL ALONG WITH YOUR MARVELLOUS TROOPS PLEASE TAKE ME ALONG.* It was signed, ***SWISS KRISSLY YOURS LOUIS SATCHMO ARMSTRONG.***[202]

Little Rock, Arkansas, September 1957. Elizabeth Eckford one of the students barred from entering the Central High School by State troops

The immediate effect on Armstrong was that the University of Alabama cancelled a concert he was scheduled to give, and Sammy Davis Jr. attacked him on television for not having spoken out on race earlier. Others said he should have joined protest marches. Armstrong's answer, given some years later after race riots in Selma, Alabama, was *They'd hit Jesus if he were black and fainting in the street . . . Luther King, whom I know very well, is a magnificient man. But my mission is music. If I demonstrated, they'd smash my face in so I couldn't play the trumpet any more.*[203] He must have got some idea of the risks he was already running when, in February 1957, he played a concert for a segregated audience of whites and blacks in Knoxville, Tennessee, and a stick of dynamite exploded outside the building after being hurled from a passing car. A White Citizens Council was suspected of the bombing: when the audience heard it, Armstrong calmed them by saying *It's all right, folks – it's just the phone.*[204] The incident was recorded in the Federal Bureau of Investigation file on Armstrong which the writer Gary Giddins requested under the American Freedom of Information Act 'and was surprised to discover that the G-men had started tracking him in 1948, when his name appeared in the address book of someone they considered suspect.'[205] Other items in the file include allegations of communist sympathies and assertions of patriotism.

In spite of the cancellation of the Soviet tour, the State Department could not afford to end its connection with Armstrong, whom it saw as a major weapon in the propaganda Cold War. As the European powers began to relinquish their colonies in Africa and Asia, and their powerful trading influences in South America, the State Department discovered that jazz could touch the hearts and minds of newly-liberated peoples. The point was powerfully made in 1956 on Armstrong's first visit to Africa on the eve of the Gold Coast's transformation from a British colony into independent Ghana. Armstrong and the All Stars found themselves playing an open-air concert to an enthusiastic crowd estimated locally at 100,000 and by the Associated Press at over half a million. At an indoor concert where a smaller crowd included Kwame Nkrumah, Armstrong announced *We'd like to lay this next one on the Prime Minister . . . 'Black and Blue'*. The journey to the Gold Coast, which Armstrong believed was the home of his ancestors, was the centrepiece of a TV special and an hour-long documentary film, 'Satchmo the Great', both made by CBS with commentary by the veteran reporter Ed Murrow.

Between them Glaser and the State Department kept the All Stars on the world stage. Arvell Shaw said: 'We were much younger then, and Armstrong was fit: no way could we have done the touring now. We'd be on the road, sometimes we wouldn't

Armstong and the All Stars performing in Accra; Ed Hall is in the check shirt.

see home for like nine months. We'd come to Europe and stay for three months. Every year we toured around the world. It was an international band. We played all over the world, we played in the most advanced technological societies like America and Japan, then in the developing nations like Africa and South America, and no matter what the culture or the race of the people, in Bombay or Botswana or Boston the people reacted the same way to the same thing. He walked on stage and unfolded that handkerchief – I guess what they recognised was a warm, honest, sincere, great human being.'[206]

On a 1960 tour of the emergent African nations, jointly financed by the State Department and Pepsi-Cola, the All Stars arrived in the middle of the civil war in the former Belgian Congo, now Congo. Shaw said: 'We landed at Leopoldville four days after Patrice Lumumba was assassinated. Both sides came together to the concert and enjoyed it and as soon as we left they started in again shooting at each other. The American ambassador said: "Louis, if we had you all the time there wouldn't be no war." That's how he got the name Ambassador Satch.'[207] The white South African government, though, banned him from entering.

Near the end of the same tour, Velma Middleton had a stroke during an open-air concert. 'Right away they took her to this funny little hospital. They didn't have the facilities to treat someone like that,' said Barney Bigard, who was back in the band. 'I'll never forgive Joe Glaser and Louis for that, because they said it would take too many people to lift her on to the plane to France. I said to myself, "This woman gave her all, and they just leave her here, like that, in some little African town."'[208] Velma died later in Sierra Leone at the age of 43.

Few of Armstrong's hundreds of foreign appearances seem to have led to the sort of violence that would become commonplace in the rock 'n' roll era. The report in the leading West German jazz magazine on what happened at Hamburg on 17 October 1955 compared it with a Nazi beerhall brawl. The All Stars arrived late for the first of two concerts at the Ernst Merck Halle, a boxing arena, and had difficulties with the public address system in front of a noisy crowd of six or seven thousand. They struggled through to a well-received performance of 'Royal Garden Blues'. 'But when the public realised that this had brought the concert to an end, all hell broke loose. The majority of the listeners began to shout and whistle, one saw umbrellas and hats flying. In shirt sleeves, Louis did give an encore, but even after that they rampaged on. Adolescents stood on the seats and howled and shouted. When after about twenty minutes an empty bottle was thrown on the stage, the rowdies began to smash up the seats, and to demolish drums, piano and bass on stage with well-aimed missiles. When a police detachment appeared, it came to a regular battle between the rabble, police and ushers. Twenty-three people were placed under provisional arrest. The hall looked like a field of rubble. The second evening performance had to be cancelled.'[209] The correspondent of the French publication *Jazz Magazine* reported that, taking into account a 20-minute intermission, the band had been on stage for less than an hour. When they tried to placate the crowd by playing encores, the promoter stopped them because 5,000 ticket-holders were waiting outside for the second house. He called the police, who moved in with rubber truncheons. 'Fighting went on for four hours and spread into all the neighbouring streets. At the end of the battle, the whole hall was in chaos, seating and windows were destroyed and 64 people had been taken to hospital with serious injuries.'[210] The reports blame greedy promoters who were rushing the All Stars from town to town to maximise profits, and attracting rowdy audiences who were led to expect a funfair rather than a jazz concert.

Any man in his mid-50s would expect the constant travel to be exhausting, and many of the All Stars soon tired of the road. But Armstrong, apart from occasional problems with his

Dr Alexander Schiff with Armstrong

lip and a series of ulcer attacks which cleared up around 1950, showed few signs of health problems. He prided himself on being *physic-minded* as a result of Mayann's teaching: what that meant was to take huge doses of laxative, at first Pluto Water and later the famous Swiss Kriss herbal mixture. He continued to eat salty food and then put himself on crash diets to lose weight. But at Lucille's insistence he had begun to bring a doctor with him on foreign tours by the time he arrived at Spoleto in Italy for the annual Festival of Two Worlds in June 1959. Alexander Schiff, the doctor for the New York State

Boxing Commission, was a friend of Glaser's and took on the job of looking after Louis. Early one morning he was called to Armstrong's bedroom and found that his lungs were filled with fluid. He took him to a local hospital, hoping that it was a chest infection, but it turned out to be a heart attack. Dr Schiff told reporters that Armstrong had pneumonia, fearing that talk of heart trouble would harm bookings. He ordered Armstrong to rest in bed, but his patient got up after a week, spent a night at Bricktop's club in Rome and flew back to New York. Only days after the attack he turned up by surprise at a charity concert and played for 15 minutes.

La Vie en Rose

Apart from a brief period with Victor, much of which coincided with a second recording ban by James Petrillo, Armstrong had been making records exclusively for Decca since his return from Europe in 1935. But Jack Kapp, the company's founder and Glaser's friend, died in 1949 and when Armstrong's contract ended in 1954, Glaser took the bold step of keeping Armstrong as a freelance. Now anyone with a song to sell could hire him, provided they could pay the price. Decca continued to record singles with novelty material and big-band arrangements in the hope of finding a hit.

Columbia had pioneered long-playing records, and their producer George Avakian had pioneered the jazz album when it was some 78s gathered into a folder. He found an ideal opportunity for Armstrong in an album of compositions by W C Handy, the 'Father of the Blues', by that time in his 80s and blind. 'St Louis Blues', which was part of the All Stars' repertoire, gets an extended and impressive performance nearly nine minutes long to open the record. Other songs had been forgotten since the days of the blues craze, and they inspire Louis and the band to some of their finest work, with assistance from Avakian's liking for the tape-splicing and over-dubbing impossible on wax but readily done on tape. On 'Atlanta Blues', for instance, Armstrong plays a trumpet obbligato on his first vocal chorus, and scats behind his own voice on the second. The Handy album was followed by one almost as good of Fats Waller tunes. On 'Blue Turning Gray Over You' he raises his trumpet with miraculous speed to follow his solo, thanks to a tape splice, and there are two Armstrongs singing together on 'I've Got a

Feeling I'm Falling'. The albums are pleasurable because Barrett Deems's drumming is looser, less heavy-handed (and footed) than usual.

In spite of some grumbling from jazz purists about the technical tricks, the records were well received and Avakian planned a series of similar tribute albums, but Glaser raised Armstrong's price and Columbia backed away. The label did, however, provide Armstrong with the hit Glaser wanted, by recording 'Mack the Knife', a song that would stay with him for the rest of his career. Once again, Avakian's ingenuity allows Armstrong to play an obbligato to his vocal. With that safely in the can, Avakian brought Lotte Lenya, widow of the composer Kurt Weill, up to the microphone to record a duet version. Tapes of the rehearsal, issued many years later, expose her uncertain intonation and, more surprisingly, her unfamiliarity with syncopation of the simplest kind. Time after time, with help from the rest of the band, Louis takes her through the phrase 'Now that Mackie's (*rest*) back in town.' Time and again she comes in early. 'It was all rather strange to her,' Avakian wrote.[211] Armstrong good-humouredly carries on the lessons until she gets it right and they produce a version that Avakian can turn into a usable take. Armstrong's own record raced up the charts until it was overtaken by Bobby Darin's up-tempo version. In the 50s no singer could be sure of having a song exclusively, and Armstrong's earlier hit with 'Blueberry Hill' had been similarly leap-frogged by Fats Domino.

George Avakian, born in Russia in 1919 as a member of an Armenian family, grew up in New York and worked as a pianist and critic. While still a student of English at Yale in 1939–40 he produced Decca's groundbreaking album 'Chicago Jazz' and reissues of out-of-print 78s including Louis's Hot Fives for Columbia. After war service he began a professional career at Columbia, starting their LP reissues of jazz classics and signing up Miles Davis and Dave Brubeck.

Over on the West Coast another producer, Norman Granz, was launching what would prove to be a four-year campaign to record Ella Fitzgerald in the best popular and show songs from the 1920s onward for his monumental series of 'song books'. Paying particular attention to lyrics, and with newly written big-band arrangements, they set a standard of quality which could not be approached by producers who were hunting a hit single.

Granz recruited Armstrong to join Fitzgerald in three albums, putting him in touch with repertoire of a sophistication more refined than he had encountered since the end of his OKeh period in 1931. In their album of songs from 'Porgy and Bess', the singers seem detached from the material and overpowered by Russ Garcia's Hollywood big band, though the 'Summertime', supported quietly by strings, is a magical exception. But the sessions with Oscar Peterson's trio, augmented by a drummer, are often charming collaborations: even if the stars may have occasionally made an uncomfortable compromise in search of a key that would suit both, they approach the songs conversationally with none of the leering that mars Armstrong's duets with Velma Middleton. The rhythm section is propulsive rather than relaxed, and more unified in the later sessions at which Louie Bellson plays elegant drums in place of Buddy Rich. Armstrong made some similar sessions without Fitzgerald – once again the Oscar Peterson Trio outshines the Russ Garcia Band.

Norman Granz (1918–2001) was a young Hollywood film editor when he started running jam sessions which led to a benefit concert at the Los Angeles Philharmonic Auditorium in 1944. It began a series of national and international tours under the title 'Jazz at the Philharmonic', which featured soloists such as Lester Young and Charlie Parker and were famous for their rabble-rousing climaxes. Granz founded the Clef, Norgran, Verve and Pablo labels, discovered the pianist Oscar Peterson and managed him and Ella Fitzgerald before retiring to Switzerland.

Ella Fitzgerald with an admiring Dizzy Gillespie during a tour in 1946. On bass is Ray Brown later Ella's husband.

Decca had got used to the idea of long-playing records by the mid-1950s and were producing what would now be called concept albums, generally with Sy Oliver's arrangements. 'Louis and the Good Book' is obviously a collection of spirituals: Oliver's two-beat style does not always fit Louis's four-beat timing. 'Louis and the Angels' is less transparent: it consists of songs with the word 'angel' in the title or the text and although the choir can make you feel queasy, the trumpet is masterly. Oliver also arranged some hit singles, including 'La Vie en Rose' and 'C'est Si Bon': the great bassist George Duvivier, who played with everyone from André Previn to Zero Mostel, was on the session: 'Louis was amazing. There was very little rehearsal. He just came in, put on his glasses, looked at his part, ran it through briefly, and said in that voice of his, *Okay. Let's make it, men!* And that was it. Perfect!'[212]

Meanwhile Gordon Jenkins arranged most of the Decca singles, and some of them are fun: in 'Chloe' the choir call out 'Louie! Louie!' from the swamp instead of 'Chloe! Chloe!' 'The Whiffenpoof Song' has lame new lyrics by Leonard Feather, turning it into 'The Boppenpoof Song', an attack on the modernists and their drug habits. From the table up at Birdland, Armstrong tells us, *all the boppers are assembled, and when they're really high, they constitute a weird personnel: They're poor little cats who have lost their way* . . . and so on. It was Armstrong's riposte for Gillespie's hilarious 'Pops' Confessin'', made nearly two years before, which parodies Armstrong's mannerisms: Gillespie holds back a couple of bars before his first entry, and ends an Armstrong-like series of high notes with a whistle. Whether there was any real animosity between them or not, it was dispelled on a TV show in 1959 when they played in public together for the first time, showing that Armstrong 'recognised that there didn't have to be any competition between Dixieland and modern jazz,' said Gillespie. 'But to let it be known that neither of us had given up his own brand of jazz, Pops and I played "The Umbrella Man" and battled it out, "Dixie" versus "modern".'[213]

The truce between the factions came as jazz and the popular music based on it was under siege from the forces of rock in the United States, while apparently enjoying a victory in northern Europe, where some revivalists had transformed themselves into commercial successes in the Trad Boom, 'trad' being shorthand for 'traditional jazz'. They wore funny hats and clothes and used the same line-up of instruments as the All Stars, with the addition of one: the banjo.

The Dukes of Dixieland wore striped blazers, sometimes plaid ones, they had a banjo, and they played resort towns like Reno and Las Vegas, so it came as a shock when Armstrong started to record with them in 1959. But in fact these are some of the best of his late recordings. The kernel of the band was the Assunto family, from New Orleans, with 'Papa' Jac Assunto playing not-too-heavy banjo and his son Freddie some unsubtle trombone: only occasionally, as in 'Canal Street Blues', does the rhythm section become too insistent. The leader was another son, the trumpeter Frank Assunto, a player of real talent if not at Bobby Hackett's level, and an excellent foil for Armstrong. The recording by Audio Fidelity, a small 'hi-fi' label, was designed to exploit stereo, then still a novelty, and separates the trumpets: Frank purrs his lyrical solos into the left channel and Louis, in a more open acoustic, fires away at the other, but Frank is not over-awed: on 'Sweethearts on Parade' his vocal pulls the rhythm about more than Armstrong does. Armstrong pulls out a storming solo on 'Sugar Foot Stomp', and the whole session is an example of his enjoyment of working alongside another trumpet, or a trombone-player closely attuned to his style, as Teagarden always had been and as Trummy Young became.

The impact of the Trad Banjo in Britain was described by the writer and agent Jim Godbolt: 'The inflexible sound of the instrument – at least as played by local musicians – dominated both the phrasing of the front line and the rhythm section.

Other characteristics of a successful and rigidly applied formula were tearaway tempos, hand-clapping on the beat by the front line and throaty vocals, superficially derived from Louis Armstrong but more redolent of the Saturday-night pub per-

former.'[214] While purists such as Ken Colyer clung to revivalism, and individualists such as Humphrey Lyttelton, Sandy Brown and Chris Barber swam into the mainstream style derived from small-band swing, hundreds of opportunists jumped aboard the trad showboat, wearing bowler hats, straw boaters, Confederate uniforms, striped trousers or fancy waistcoats, almost all sounding the same and almost all to be swept away by the tidal wave from the Mersey.

Glaser's other major jazz client at the time was the pianist Dave Brubeck, a favourite of the college crowd and a big seller for Columbia. Offended by prejudice which kept his own mixed-race quartet out of the South, Brubeck was shocked to hear that a restaurant owner in supposedly enlightened Connecticut had humiliated Armstrong by refusing to let him use his lavatory. Brubeck and his wife Iola wrote a musical about the disgraceful behaviour of some Americans to their envoy to the world. 'The Real Ambassadors' is worthy rather than exciting – its only public performance was at a jazz festival. On the recording, Louis is often reduced from a major international star to a performer in a San Francisco coffee house by having to sing lyrics (to 'Cultural Exchange') such as

When our neighbours call us vermin
We send them Woody Herman.

But he manages to bring some meaning to the plodding pastoral 'Summer Song', which earned it a revival as a soundtrack for a television commercial forty years later.

Armstrong went to France to appear and play in a film, 'Paris Blues', with Paul Newman and Sidney Poitier as expatriate musicians: Armstrong, not surprisingly, plays a trumpeter. Ellington wrote the score and recorded Armstrong's solos with studio players, American and local, in Paris. One of them gives us the last chance to hear him with a top-class big band and he plays well on it, but sadly the composition is a characterless flag-waver. The Ellington authority Eddie Lambert wondered what the result would have been if they had met (apart from the trans-continental radio collaboration in 1945) when Armstrong was at his peak, and concluded: 'An Ellington score behind one of Armstrong's great solos might have been an unnecessary enrichment, while a soloist of Armstrong's blazing genius in an Ellington score might well have distracted the listener from the writing.'[215]

When Armstrong and Ellington got a chance to make a protracted recording together for Roulette Records, a few months after the movie, it was with the All Stars: the ex-Ellington clarinet-player Barney Bigard was back in the personnel, and Ellington had stolen Billy Kyle's gig, as he used to joke. They played 16 Ellington standards and one song which Ellington claimed to have written with Armstrong in mind 20 years before, 'Azalea'. Because Michael Cuscuna, a specialist in reconstructing taped sessions, has pieced together and reissued the Armstrong–Ellington recordings, we have a clear picture of what happened in the studio on East 24th Street in Manhattan on 3 and 4 April 1961. Everybody is relaxed and in good humour, but works with the utmost concentration: Trummy Young discards all the rough tone he sometimes used in the All Stars, and plays with a suave sound and sly, modern phrasing; Bigard, perhaps feeling sure of his ground with them, embraces Ellington's tunes positively; the young drummer Danny Barcelona, who normally rushed the beat and threatened to destabilise performances, holds himself steady; Mort Herbert, the bass-player, imaginatively tackles the exposure Ellington sometimes gives him when he pares down his piano parts. Ellington gently commands the sessions, his piano subdued but supportive, the tempos moderate, the dynamic range limited so that Armstrong's burnished tone can shine above it. His cooperative studio manner contrasts with his playing on a television show later, when he and the All Stars met again and performed two of the same numbers: for the later performance Ellington abandons his improvisatory group-minded playing and reproduces on the piano large sections of his orchestral arrangements – perhaps the sketches for the studio recordings had been lost in the intervening nine months.

'The majestic sound and noble accents he clothes it in here should serve as a lesson to those who – still – speak of his decline.'

–*Dan Morgenstern*[216]

Throughout the meeting with Ellington, Armstrong is magnificent, in spite of – or perhaps because of – having had only a few of the themes on even the fringe of his repertoire. 'Azalea' is only a partial success: there is a fine trumpet solo, but the vocal is fatally damaged by the lyrics, written by Ellington himself in his most scented mode, and including such undigested crudities as rhyming the title with 'avail ya''. But Louis imparts a snarling ferocity to 'Black and Tan Fantasy'. It is so much a composition for Ellington's own band that Armstrong had no reason to have ever played it before, but he clearly knows the routine. And, as the critic Dan Morgenstern pointed out, he turns it into his own by incorporating his 1928 blues, 'Muggles'. Young contributes a threatening plunger solo, sustaining the mood Armstrong sets.

Few people now can remember seeing Armstrong with a big band, so the images that endure belong to the All Stars era. As it drew to a close, we remember his big flat feet plodding down to the microphone; the white handkerchief, used not so much to dab at his forehead as to wipe across his mouth between trumpet solo and vocal; the introspective pout of his lips before beginning to sing; his gestures while singing or talking (almost all made by his right hand because the trumpet was being carried in the left) with the thumb and little finger spread out and the other fingers close together as if ready to clamp down again on the three valves; his vast smile, looking broader than ever as his face thinned and narrowed.

He often looked frail next to his sidemen, particularly the enormous trombonist 'Big Chief' Russell Moore who followed Young into what was probably the weakest edition of the All Stars. Moore himself was an adroit technician with a tendency to raucousness; his front-line partner was Joe Darensbourg, who used an ugly gas-pipe tone and specialised in slap-tonguing, a method almost abandoned by clarinet-players in the middle 1920s. But

Tyree Glenn (1912–74) worked in local bands in his native Texas and moved to the West Coast before joining Cab Calloway in New York. After a post-war visit to Europe he joined Duke Ellington to take over the plunger trombone chair left vacant by the death of the great Tricky Sam Nanton. 'A very beautiful trombone player,' Ellington called him, and 'a very agile-minded musician'.[217] Glenn also worked as an actor, played vibraphone, and became musical director for the All Stars.

Armstrong told the cornetist Ruby Braff: *I work with two bands, the one on the stage and the one in my head. If they sound good on stage, OK, I'll play with them. If not, I just turn up the volume of the band in my head.*[218] Darensbourg gave way to Eddie Shu, then Armstrong's old swimming buddy Buster Bailey, and finally to Joe Muranyi. Billy Kyle's death brought Marty Napoleon back on piano and the trombone job went to Tyree Glenn, another man-mountain, with whom Louis performed the sort of comedy routines he had done with Velma Middleton. Tyree wore a woman's hat for their duet on 'That's My Desire'.

In 1967 'What a Wonderful World', a song Armstrong liked, was a runaway hit in Europe, reaching the top of the British charts. (It was a flop on its release in the United States – 17 years later it was No. 1 there, having been used on the soundtrack of 'Good Morning, Vietnam'.) The following June, Armstrong brought the All Stars to Batley, near Leeds, for two weeks at the 1,600-seat Variety Club, an up-market version of a working men's club. Humphrey Lyttelton heard reports that there was little left of his trumpet-playing: 'Some days later, I was astonished to arrive at the club a few minutes late after tearing up from an engagement in Leeds to hear the familiar solo in "Indiana", rippling high notes and all, blasting out across the huge auditorium.'[219]

Back in New York Armstrong went to see his doctor, Gary Zucker, who ordered him into hospital with heart and kidney problems and shortness of breath. His relentless touring and smoking – either marijuana or Camels – had damaged the lungs he was always so proud of having developed through swimming, in spite of his being what Arvell Shaw called 'a health nut'.[220] One reporter described his idiosyncratic health routine: 'He takes his nightly laxative, swallows thirteen vitamin tablets in one gulp several times a day, sprays himself with Chanel No. 5, sucks special throat sweets, brushes his chest with liniment and keeps his calloused lips oiled with salve.'[221]

Shaw added: 'He would go out every now and again with Lucille, and have a beer or two to drink, but he didn't do anything to excess . . . He took care of himself: that's the only way he could have survived, as hard as he worked for that many years. If he had taken things a little easier he could have lasted another five, or six or maybe another ten years, but that wasn't Louis. Each time he walked on the stage he gave the best that he could possibly give.'[222] But he was also eating ham hocks with red beans and rice, in spite of being ordered on to a salt-free diet.

Instead of heeding Dr Zucker, Armstrong vanished for a fortnight – his movements remain a mystery, but he is supposed to have headed for Harlem and spent the time eating, smoking and gambling among old friends and fans. When he returned, bloated from his kidneys' failure to cope with fluid, Dr Zucker sent him to Beth Israel Hospital and prescribed diuretics to stabilise his metabolism. He was able to leave hospital, but in February 1969 he was back. He had to have a tracheostomy to remove fluid from his lungs. Recovering in his bed at Beth Israel on 31 March 1969,

Armstrong was deprived of his beloved typewriter, so he picked up a pen when he began to reminisce about his childhood, the Karnovsky family and other Jews, such as Dr Zucker, who had shown kindness to him, sometimes when African-Americans had not. He wrote:

I dedicate this book
to my manager and pal
Mr. Joe Glaser
The best Friend
That I've ever had
May the Lord Bless Him
Watch over him always.

His boy & disciple who loved him dearly.
Louis
Satchmo
Armstrong

He did not know that Glaser was also a patient in Beth Israel. He had been found in the lift to his penthouse, standing motionless as it went up and down after having a massive stroke. Armstrong's doctors and Lucille decided that the knowledge would endanger Armstrong's own health, and he found out only when Dizzy Gillespie called in on him after giving blood for Glaser, who was in a coma. Then he insisted on being taken in his wheelchair to see Glaser in intensive care. Afterwards he told Lucille: *I went down to see him and he didn't know me.*[223] Glaser did not recover from the coma: he died on 6 June. 'In some mysterious way, Joe's will made Armstrong a rich man,' Ernie Anderson wrote; Lucille explained that Glaser had taken half of Armstrong's fees, as his partner. 'She was not so pleased to learn that the agency had taken another 15 per cent commission from

Armstrong's half. Still, Louis's share amounted to a considerable sum. He told Bobby Hackett, who was very close to him, that it amounted to *a bit more than two million dollars*. It was not all in cash, one item was a piece of prime real estate on Rodeo Drive in Beverly Hills.'[224]

Warned off the trumpet and touring by his doctors, Armstrong had to spend more time at the house in Corona with 'The Armstrongs' on the doormat, among the tape boxes he had decorated with collages of publicity pictures and press cuttings, stuck down with strips of Scotch tape. The recordings in them were mainly made in his den at home, chatting and bickering with Lucille and entertaining guests, or in dressing rooms on the road, picking up local radio stations and singing or playing along with them, or holding court with visitors and telling them jokes, often dirty. He indexed music by the last name of the artist or title, so 'In the Mood' and 'All by Myself' are in the same list as records by trombonist Benny Morton.

In October 1969 he flew to London and recorded the main title song for a James Bond picture, 'On Her Majesty's Secret Service', a John Barry composition, 'We Have All the Time in the World', which became another of Armstrong's performances to re-emerge in later years as the soundtrack for a television commercial. Producers now had to find songs through which he could make an impact – and perhaps a hit – without much help from his trumpet, and they retreated into novelty material. In May 1970 he recorded an album of oddly assorted inspirational songs in a New York studio full of guests, including Miles Davis, Ornette Coleman, Tony Bennett, Eddie Condon and Bobby Hackett. One of the tunes was a remake of 'What a Wonderful World'. George Duvivier, who played bass, said: 'When we listened to the playback, there wasn't a dry eye in the studio. He was too weak to play, which was sad. But he remained the consummate artist to the end.'[225] He also managed to make fun of the flower-power sanctimony of 'Give Peace a Chance' by subverting the lyrics: *Give a piece,* he sang, *give a BIG piece . . .* Even a country and western album had the occasional flash of humour as he struggled with a lumpy Nashville rhythm section and unsympathetic lyrics. 'Almost Persuaded' gives him an opportunity to change the words so that he sings: *I'd like to kiss those strange chops.*

Armstrong appeared on TV shows and in a charity concert in London; he took the All Stars to Las Vegas and, against medical advice, into the Empire Room at the Waldorf Astoria Hotel in New York. Unable to play, barely able to walk, needing help to get on and off stage, Armstrong insisted on fulfilling his contract. Arvell Shaw was with the All Stars and the Waldorf's house band of hard-bitten New York veterans: 'There was an 18-piece band playing for the show and they all had tears in their eyes. At the end of the engagement, Louis went back into hospital and six weeks later he was dead. It was like the loss of a member of my family.'[226]

Armstrong went home from Beth Israel Hospital in time to celebrate his birthday on 4 July. He had planned another outing with the All Stars. On 6 July 1971, at 5.30 in the morning, he died in his sleep.

His body lay in state at the red-brick castle of the 7th Regiment National Guard Armory at Park Avenue and 66th Street in Manhattan, and 25,000 people filed past on 8 July. Next day his funeral was held at the little Corona Congregational Church. 'If Joe Glaser had been alive Louis would have had a grand send-off,' said Dan Morgenstern, who was then editor of *Down Beat* magazine. 'But Lucille wanted to be respectable and had ties to the community – she was under some pressure to have it there.'[227]

'I loved and respected Louis Armstrong. He was born poor, died rich, and never hurt anyone on the way.'

–Duke Ellington[228]

Armstrong's coffin on the way to Flushing Cemetery

Morgenstern and 5,000 other people waited outside while Peggy Lee sang 'The Lord's Prayer' and Al Hibbler sang 'The Saints'. A congregation of 500, including Governor Nelson Rockefeller, New York Mayor John Lindsay, Dizzy Gillespie, Guy Lombardo, and the avant-garde saxophonist Ornette Coleman, who had slipped past the doormen, fanned themselves in the 95-degree heat with Martin Luther King memorial fans in an attempt to cool. Armstrong was buried in Flushing Cemetery. In New Orleans 15,000 people joined a parade.

'He was a wise man. He had a brilliant mind: very little formal education, but brilliant.'

—Arvell Shaw[229]

Lucille stayed on in the house in Corona, living quietly and working to preserve her husband's memory, although she turned his den into a sitting room. In October 1983 she went to Boston for a fund-raising concert. She had a seizure in her hotel room and died in hospital on 5 October, aged 69. Lucille was buried next to her husband. She left the house to the City of New York as a memorial: along with the archive of recordings and mementos which Armstrong left behind; it is now in the care of Queens College/City University of New York. His adopted home town named a tennis stadium after him next to the one named after the black champion Arthur Ashe. Down in New Orleans they named the airport after him, and put up a statue of him in Louis Armstrong Park, next to the place which had once been Congo Square. At the entrance they put his name in lights.

Notes:

The three books published under Louis Armstrong's name are abbreviated in the notes as follows:

LA, *Swing*: Louis Armstrong, *Swing That Music*
LA, *Life*: Louis Armstrong, Satchmo: *My Life in New Orleans*
LA, *Words*: *Louis Armstrong In His Own Words*.

1   Alan Lomax, *Mr Jelly Roll*, 1950: Virgin Books edition, p. 277
2   Mark Twain, *Life on the Mississippi*, 1883: Airmont edition, p. 205
3   LA, *Life*, p. 9
4   LA, *Life*, p. 9
5   LA, *Life*, p. 10
6   LA, *Life*, p. 12
7   LA, *Life*, p. 14
8   LA, *Life*, p. 13
9   LA, *Life*, p. 16
10 H L Mencken, *The American Language*, supplement 1, New York 1945, p. 597
11 LA, *Words*, pp. 8–9
12 LA, *Words*, p. 22
13 LA, *Words*, p. 14
14 LA, *Words*, p. 15
15 Mary Ellin Barrett, *Irving Berlin: A Daughter's Memoir*, New York 1995, p. 62.
16 LA, *Swing*, p. 5
17 Quoted in Lawrence Bergreen, *Louis Armstrong: An Extravagant Life*, New York and London, 1997, p. 69

18 LA, *Words*, p. 122
19 LA, *Life*, p. 44
20 LA, *Life*, p. 42
21 LA, *Life*, pp. 45–6
22 LA, *Life*, p. 46
23 Sidney Bechet, *Treat it Gentle*, London 1960, p. 6
24 Samuel B Charters, *Jazz New Orleans 1894–1963*, revised edition New York 1953, p. 18
25 Alan Lomax, *Mr Jelly Roll*, p. 54
26 Quoted in Jack V Buerkle and Danny Barker, *Bourbon Street Black*, New York 1973, p. 17
27 LA, *Words*, p. 24
28 LA, *Words*, p. 24
29 LA, *Words*, p. 88
30 Bechet, *Treat it Gentle*, p. 98
31 Martin Williams, *Jazz Masters of New Orleans*, New York and London 1967, p. 171
32 Max Jones and John Chilton, *Louis: The Louis Armstrong Story 1900–1971*, revised edition, London 1975, p. 89

33 LA, *Words*, p. 89

34 LA, *Words*, p. 28

35 Pops Foster, *The Autobiography of a New Orleans Jazzman*, as told to Tom Stoddard, Berkeley, California, 1971, p. 113

36 A detailed account is in Dr Bruce Boyd Raeburn's internet exhibit, Riverboats and Jazz, at www.tulane.edu/~lmiller/raeburn/

37 LA, *Swing*, p. 47

38 LA, *Swing*, p. 56

39 Richard M Sudhalter, *Lost Chords*, New York 1999, p. 188

40 LA, *Swing*, pp. 53–4

41 Baby Dodds, *The Baby Dodds Story*, as told to Larry Gara, revised editon, Baton Rouge, Louisiana, 1992, p.24.

42 LA, *Swing*, p. 55

43 LA, *Life*, p. 206

44 Gary Giddins, *Satchmo: The Genius of Louis Armstrong*, revised edition, New York 2001, p. 155

45 Quoted in Jones and Chilton, *Louis*, p. 79

46 Nat Shapiro and Nat Hentoff, *Hear Me Talkin' to Ya*, New York 1955, p. 103

47 Mervyn Sorenson, quoted by Mark Berresford in 'A Visit To Richmond in 1922', *Storyville*, Oct–Nov 1983

48 Williams, *Jazz Masters of New Orleans*, p. 99

49 *Chicago Defender*, 16 February 1924, quoted in Wright et al. Joe King Oliver, Chigwell, 1976.

50 LA, *Words*, p. 90

51 LA, *Words*, p. 90

52 Rex Stewart, *Jazz Masters of the Thirties*, New York 1972, p. 40

53 *Record Changer*, July–Aug 1950, p. 15

54 *Record Changer*, July–Aug 1950, p. 15

55 Transcribed in Edward Brooks, *The Young Louis Armstrong on Records*, Lanham, MD, and London 2002, p. 142

56 Interview with Fred Rabell quoted in Giddins, *Satchmo*, p. 54

57 Jones and Chilton, *Louis*, p. 236

58 Foster, *Autobiography*, p. 100

59 Ernie Anderson, 'Louis Armstrong: a personal memoir', *Storyville*, 1 December 1991

60 Tom Lord, *Clarence Williams*, Chigwell 1976, p. 122

61 LA, *Words*, p. 93

62 Stewart, *Jazz Masters of the Thirties*, p. 44

63 Interview by Lester Koenig, *Record Changer*, July–August 1950

64 Mezz Mezzrow with Bernard Wolfe, *Really the Blues*, New York 1946, paperback edition 1993, p. 120

65 LA, *Words*, p. 132

66 *Record Changer*, July–August 1950

67 LA, *Words*, p. 128

68 Richard Hadlock, *Jazz Masters of the Twenties*, New York 1965, p. 37

69 LA, *Words*, p. 94

70 LA, *Words*, p. 95
71 William Russell, in
    Frederic Ramsey, Jr. and
    Charles Edward Smith,
    Jazzmen, New York 1939,
    paperback edition 1985,
    p. 129
72 LA, *Words*, p. 95
73 LA, *Words*, p. 95
74 LA, *Words*, p. 26
75 LA, *Words*, p. 96
76 LA, *Words*, p. 97
77 LA, *Words*, p. 98
78 Interview with author,
    3 December 2002
79 LA, *Words*, p. 100
80 Stanley Dance, *The World of
    Earl Hines*, New York
    1977, p. 53
81 Bill Berry, answering
    questions at Duke
    Ellington convention,
    Leeds, May 1997
82 Kaiser Marshall in Shapiro
    and Hentoff, *Hear Me
    Talkin' to Ya*, p. 281
83 George T. Simon, *Metronome*
    review 1942, quoted in
    Simon *The Big Bands*, New
    York 1967, p. 321
84 Quoted in John S Wilson,
    booklet for *The Life*
    re-issue of Armstrong
    recordings.
85 Richard M Sudhalter,
    *Stardust Melody: The Life
    and Music of Hoagy
    Carmichael*, New York
    2002, pp. 102, 108–13
86 Alec Wilder, *American
    Popular Song*, New York
    1972, p. 375
87 Ralph Berton, *Remembering
    Bix*, British edition
    London 1974, p. 389
88 LA, *Words*, pp. 107–8

89 LA, *Words*, p. 108
90 Interview with Dan
    Havens, *Jazz Journal
    International*, January 1992
91 LA, *Words*, p. 110
92 Jones and Chilton, *Louis*,
    p. 145
93 James, *Jazz Journal*,
    January 1992
94 LA, *Swing*, p. 99
95 Interview with author,
    8 December 2002
96 James, *Jazz Journal*,
    January 1992
97 Ronald G Welburn, 'The
    Early Record Review', in
    Dan Morgenstern, Charles
    Nanry and David A Cayer
    *(eds), Annual Review of Jazz
    Studies 3*, New Brunswick,
    NJ 1985
98 James, *Jazz Journal*,
    January 1992
99 LA, *Words*, p. 21
100 Jones and Chilton, *Louis*,
    p. 164
101 Kenneth Allsop, *Hard
    Travellin'*, London, 1967,
    p. 140
102 Teddy Wilson with Arle
    Ligthart and Humphrey
    van Loo, *Teddy Wilson
    Talks Jazz*, London 1996,
    p. 14
103 Mezzrow, *Really the Blues*,
    p. 257
104 *Daily Express*, 31 March
    1933
105 Ernie Anderson, Joe Glaser
    and Louis Armstrong,
    Storyville 160, 1 December
    1994
106 John Hammond *with
    Irving Townsend, John
    Hammond on Record*, New
    York 1977, p. 105

107 LA, *Words*, p. 160

108 Duke Ellington, *Music is My Mistress*, British edition 1974, p. 234–5

109 Interview, *Cadence*, July 1979

110 Anderson, Glaser and Armstrong, *Storyville* 160

111 Quoted in Jones and Chilton, *Louis*, p. 189

112 LA, *Words*, p. 99

113 Lionel Hampton with James Haskins: *Hamp, an autobiography*, London edition, 1990, p. 83

114 Bill Crow, *Jazz Anecdotes*, New York 1990, p. 212

115 Anderson, Glaser and Armstrong, *Storyville* 160

116 LA, *Words*, p. 185

117 John Chilton, *Ride, Red, Ride: the Life of Henry 'Red' Allen*, London 1999, p. 96

118 *Record Changer*, July–August 1950

119 LA, *Swing*, pp. 94–5

120 *Cadence*, July 1979

121 LA, *Swing*, 1993 edition, introduction, p. xii

122 Mel Powell, in Balliett, p. 210

123 Whitney Balliett, Big Sid, in *American Musicians II*, New York, 1996, p. 202

124 Balliett, p. 206

125 Giddins, *Satchmo*, p. 112

126 LA, *Words*, p. 175

127 John R T Davies, 'The Mills Brothers 1931–34', *Storyville* 6, August–September 1966

128 Gary Giddins, *Visions of Jazz*, New York 1998, p. 25

129 Henry D Spalding, *Encyclopedia of Black Folklore and Humor*, Middle Village, NY, revised edition, 1978, p. 341

130 Clarence Major (ed), *Juba to Jive, a Dictionary of African-American Slang*, New York 1994, p. 254

131 Albert McCarthy, 'The Re-emergence of Traditional Jazz', in Nat Hentoff and Albert McCarthy (eds) *Jazz: New Perspectives on the History of Jazz*, London edition 1962, p. 306

132 Bechet, *Treat it Gentle*, p. 176

133 Richard Meryman, *Louis Armstrong, a Self-Portrait*, New York 1971, p. 49

134 Chris Albertson, Time-Life album note, quoted by James Lincoln Collier, *Louis Armstrong*, New York 1983, p. 282

135 LA, *Words*, p. 99

136 LA, *Words*, p. 184

137 LA, *Words*, p. 186

138 LA, *Words*, p. 144

139 LA, *Words*, p. 160

140 LA, *Words*, p. 159

141 LA, *Words*, p. 159

142 Patricia Willard, interview with Bigard, Los Angeles 1976: in Jazz Oral History Interviews, Institute of Jazz Studies at Rutgers-Newark University. Excerpted in Joshua Berrett (ed) *A Louis Armstrong Companion*, New York 1999, p. 169

143 Interview with author, 28 May 2003

144 Speech at University of Southern California, 9 April 1972, in *Joy to the World: a*

Celebration of Satchmo, Los Angeles 1973, p. 3

145 Wilder, *American Popular Song*, p. 399

146 *New York Times*, 14 June 1956

147 Sigmund Spaeth, *A History of Popular Music in America*, New York 1948; London edition 1961, p. 540

148 John Chilton, *Sidney Bechet: the Wizard of Jazz*, London 1987, p. 161

149 Anderson, Glaser and Armstrong: *Storyville* 160

150 Anderson, Glaser and Armstrong, *Storyville* 160

151 Anderson, Glaser and Armstrong, *Storyville* 161, March 1995

152 Bob Porter and Mark Gardner, interview with Sonny Criss, *Jazz Monthly*, April 1968, quoted by Alyn Shipton in *Groovin' High*, New York 1999, p. 156.

153 Anderson, Glaser and Armstrong, *Storyville* 160

154 Marshall and Jean Stearns, *Jazz Dance*, New York 1968, p. 270

155 Patricia Willard, interview with Trummy Young in Jazz Oral History Interviews, Institute of Jazz Studies at Rutgers-Newark University. Excerpted in Berrett (ed) *A Louis Armstrong Companion*, p. 173

156 Jack Lesberg, interview by Bob Rusch, *Cadence*, June 1987

157 Ellington, *Music is My Mistress*, p. 115

158 Quoted in Balliett, 'Big T', in *American Musicians II*, New York, 1996, p. 185

159 Balliett, 'Big T', p. 187

160 Interview in *Record Changer*, July–August 1950

161 Interview in *Record Changer*, July–August 1950

162 LA, 'Scanning the History of Jazz', in *The Jazz Review*, July 1960; reprinted in LA, *Words*, p. 175.

163 *Down Beat*, 7 April 1948, quoted in Bergreen, *Louis Armstrong*, p. 440

164 Rudi Blesh, *Shining Trumpets*, New York 1946, p. 286

165 Humphrey Lyttelton, *I Play as I Please*, London 1954, p. 156

166 Humphrey Lyttelton, *Second Chorus*, London 1958, p. 144

167 Interview with author, 15 July 2002

168 Quoted by Barney Bigard in Crow, *Jazz Anecdotes*, p. 213

169 Quoted in Balliett, *American Musicians II*, p. 203

170 Dance, *World of Earl Hines*, p. 105

171 *Down Beat*, 22 February 1952

172 Interview in *Jazz Review*, February 2003

173 Interview with author, 4 September 2002

174 Red Callender and Elaine Cohen, *Unfinished Dream*, London 1985, p. 61

175 Interview with Bob Rusch, *Cadence*, June 1987

176 *Down Beat*, 1 July 1949

177 LA, *Words*, pp. 151–2

178 LA, *Life*, p. 29

179 LA, *Words*, p. 152

180 Interview with author, 15 July 2002

181 Interview, *Cadence*, May 1981

182 Interview with author, 31 July 2002

183 Crow, *Jazz Anecdotes*, pp. 213–14

184 Interview with author 31 July, 2002

185 Interview, *Cadence*, July 1987

186 Interview with author, 4 September 2002

187 Personal communication with author, 17 December 2002

188 Interview with author, 24 December 2002

189 Interview with author, 24 December 2002

190 Personal communication with author, 17 December 2002

191 Conversation with author, 29 May 2003

192 Joe Levinson, 'My Audition with Satchmo', Jazz Institute of Chicago in-line newsletter December 2002 (www.jazzinstitute-ofchicago.org/jazzgram/people/satchmo.asp)

193 Interview with author, 15 July 2002

194 Sinclair Traill, interview with Lesberg, *Jazz Journal*, September 1970

195 Crow, *Jazz Anecdotes*, p. 214

196 Interview with author, 31 July 2002

197 Lyttelton, *Take it From the Top*, London 1975, p. 153

198 Interview with author, 15 July 2002

199 Barney Bigard, ed. Barry Martyn, *With Louis and the Duke*, London 1985, p. 110

200 LA, *Words*, p. 193

201 Quoted in Giddins, *Satchmo*, p. 128

202 LA, *Words*, p. 194

203 Louis Armstrong, 1965, quoted in Carla M Weaver, 'A Tribute to Louis Armstrong', www.duke.edu/~cmw4/jazz/m

204 Reuters report in *London Evening News*, 20 February 1957

205 Giddins, *Satchmo*, p. 129

206 Interview with author, 15 July 2002

207 Interview with author, 15 July 2002

208 Bigard, *With Louis and the Duke*, p. 109

209 *Jazz Podium*, November 1955 (trans Andrew Sheppard)

210 Klaus Berenbrok, *Jazz Magazine*, December 1955 (author's translation)

211 Notes to 'Lenya Sings Weill', Sony Classical MHK 60647, 1999

212 Edward Berger, *Bassically Speaking, an oral history of George Duvivier*: Rutgers, NJ, Metuchen, NJ, and London, 1993, p. 163

213 Dizzy Gillespie with Al Fraser, *To Be or Not . . . to Bop*, New York 1979, p. 448

214 Jim Godbolt, *A History of Jazz in Britain 1919–1950*, London 1984, p. 267

215 Eddie Lambert, *Duke Ellington: A Listener's Guide*, Lanham, Maryland, and Rutgers, NJ, 1999, p. 224

216 Notes to *Roulette* 24547, 2000

217 Stanley Dance, *The World of Duke Ellington*, London 1970, p. 7

218 Braff, interviewed by Martin Gayford in *Daily Telegraph*, 20 January 2001

219 Lyttelton, *Take it From the Top*, pp. 161–2

220 Interview with author, 15 July 2002

221 Lionel Crane, 'The Wonderful World of Satchmo', *Sunday Mirror*, 23 June 1968

222 Interview with author, 15 July 2002

223 Interview with Lucille Armstrong in Collier, *Louis Armstrong*, p. 330

224 Anderson, Glaser and Armstrong, *Storyville* 161

225 Berger, *Bassically Speaking*, p. 163

226 Interview by Peter Vacher, *Jazz Journal International*, October 1983

227 Interview with author, 13 May 2003

228 Ellington, *Music is My Mistress*, p. 236

229 Interview with author, 15 July 2002

Acknowledgements

My gratitude for invaluable help with this book goes to the following people and the institutions with which they are connected: David Nathan of the National Jazz Federation Archive, Loughton, Essex; Andrew Simons, Jazz Curator, and the staff of the National Sound Archive, British Library; Dr Wolfram Knauer, Director, and staff of the Jazz-Institut Darmstadt, Germany; Gavin Henderson, Principal, Trinity College of Music, London, and Linda Hirst, Head of Vocal Studies, Trinity College of Music; Dr Bruce Boyd Raeburn, Curator, Hogan Jazz Archive, Tulane University Libraries, New Orleans, Louisiana; Dr Michael Cogswell, Director, and Peggy Alexander, Archives Curator, Louis Armstrong House and Archive, Queens College, New York.

My thanks also to the following individuals who provided valuable information or advice: Jim Beebe, Jack Bradley, Campbell Burnap, Frances Butlin, John Chilton, Charlie Crump, Elsa Davern, John R T Davies, Natasha Edwards, Selina Hastings, Andrew Lownie, William B McCredie, Stuart O'Connor, Michael and Daphne Peacock, Brian Peerless, Andy Sheppard, Chris Sheridan, Ken Vail. Dan Morgeristern, Director, and the staff of the Institute of Jazz Studies, Rutgers University, Newark, New Jersey.

Tom Lord of Lord Music Reference Inc (www.lordisco.com) kindly sent from Canada a printout of the updated Armstrong section of 'The Jazz Discography', which he compiles and publishes. Franz Hoffmann provided new material on Armstrong and the Luis Russell band before it was published in his 'Henry "Red" Allen and J C Higginbotham Collection'.

Among other old friends my particular thanks go to two clarinetists: Wally Fawkes (Trog) for his beautiful cover and Kenny Davern for his many insights, particularly on Jack Teagarden and Trummy Young, and for taking time to read the manuscript.

Russ Phillips, patiently answered my questions about his father's time with the All Stars, and his own experiences as a boy on the bus. I was also given generous amounts of time in telephone interviews by two former members of the All Stars, Joe Muranyi and the late Arvell Shaw, who regrettably died while this book was in preparation.

At Haus Publishing, Barbara Schwepcke and Robert Pritchard have been unfailingly supportive, encouraging and patient. At home my wife, Jane Mays, has been all those things and more, and to her go my thanks and love.

Needless to say, any errors are nobody's fault but mine.

Chronology

Year	History	Culture
1901	In Britain, Queen Victoria dies; Edward VII becomes king. In US, McKinley assassinated; Theodore Roosevelt becomes president. In US, instant coffee invented.	Strindberg, *The Dance of Death.* Kipling, *Kim.* Freud, *The Psychopathology of Everyday Life.* Anton Chekhov, *The Three Sisters.*
1906	In US, San Francisco earthquake leaves 1,000 dead and 200,000 homeless.	Henri Matisse, *Bonheur de vivre.* Maxim Gorky, *The Mother*
1907	Anglo-Russian Entente. Electric washing-machine invented.	Conrad, *The Secret Agent.* Rainer Maria Rilke, *Neue Gedichte.*
1913	In US, Woodrow Wilson becomes president (until 1921). 16th Amendment is passed, allowing the collection of income tax.	Stravinsky, *The Rite of Spring.* Marcel Proust, *A la recherche du temps perdu* (until 1927).
1915	In US, William J Simmons revives the Ku Klux Klan. In US, House of Representatives defeats proposal for women's suffrage. Albert Einstein introduces general theory of relativity.	John Buchan, *The Thirty-Nine Steps.* D H Lawrence, *The Rainbow.*
1917	In Russia, revolutions in February and October. Tsar Nicholas II abdicates. Communists seize power under Vladimir Lenin. US enters First World War.	First recording of New Orleans jazz, by original Dixieland Jazz Band. Franz Kafka, *Metamorphosis.* T S Eliot, *Prufrock and Other Observations.*

1918	Replaces Joe Oliver in Kid Ory's band. Works in parades with Papa Celestin's Tuxedo Brass Band and on day cruises on the Mississippi in Fate Marable's orchestra on board the steamboats of the Streckfus Line.
1919	In May Armstrong moves to St Louis for the summer season of pleasure cruises.
1921	Returns to New Orleans, working with Celestin and Henry Allen's marching bands, and in Tom Anderson's Cabaret Club and the Fernandez Club.
1922	Joe Oliver calls Armstrong to Chicago; joins the Creole Jazz Band at the Lincoln Gardens on second cornet, meeting the pianist, Lil Hardin.
1923	Oliver's band goes on a tour of the Mid-West and makes its first records in Richmond, Indiana, on 5 April.
1924	Marries Lil Hardin on 5 February. Lil buys a house and Clarence comes to live with them. In June, Louis quits Oliver and joins Fletcher Henderson's Orchestra in New York in October. He records with Henderson, Clarence Williams and the blues singers Ma Rainey, Alberta Hunter and Sippie Wallace.
1925	Recordings with Bessie Smith, Clara Smith and Trixie Smith. In November, Armstrong leaves Henderson, returns to Chicago to join his wife's Dreamland Syncopators, and makes his first records as leader, with the Hot Five. He appears with Erskine Tate's Orchestra at a big cinema, the Vendome Theater, as a featured soloist between movies.
1926	Records 'Heebie Jeebies' with scat vocal. Leaves Lil's band and joins Carroll Dickerson at the Sunset Café, while still appearing at the Vendome, where he meets Alpha Smith and begins an affair.

1918	In Russia, Tsar Nicholas II and family executed. 11 November: Armistice agreement ends First World War. British take Palestine and Syria. In UK, women over 30 get right to vote. 'Spanish flu' epidemic kills at least 20m people in Europe, US and India.	Oswald Spengler, *The Decline of the West*, Volume 1. Amédée Ozenfant and Le Corbusier, *Après le Cubisme*. Paul Klee, *Gartenplan*. *Tarzan of the Apes* with Elmo Lincoln.
1919	Treaty of Versailles. Comintern held in Moscow. In US, Prohibition adopted, is to be introduced in 1920. Irish Civil War (until 1921).	The Bauhaus founded in Weimar. United Artists formed with Charlie Chaplin, Mary Pickford, Douglas Fairbanks and D W Griffith as partners.
1921	National Economic Policy in Soviet Union. In China, Communist Party founded.	Sergey Prokofiev, *The Love for Three Oranges*. Chaplin, *The Kid*.
1922	Benito Mussolini's fascists march on Rome. First supermarket opens in San Francisco.	T S Eliot, *The Waste Land*. Joyce, *Ulysses*.
1923	In US, President Harding dies suddenly, succeeded by Calvin Coolidge.	Le Corbusier, *Vers une architecture*.
1924	Vladimir Lenin dies. In US, Johnson-Reed Act reduces European immigration and bans Japanese.	Forster, *A Passage to India*. Thomas Mann, *The Magic Mountain*. André Breton, first surrealist manifesto.
1925	Pact of Locarno. Chiang Kai-shek launches campaign to unify China. Discovery of ionosphere. In US, Scopes Trial.	F Scott Fitzgerald, *The Great Gatsby*. Kafka, *The Trial*. Adolf Hitler, *Mein Kampf* (Vol. 1). Sergey Eisenstein, *Battleship Potemkin*. Television invented.
1926	Germany joins League of Nations. Antonio Gramsci imprisoned in Italy. France establishes Republic of Lebanon. Hirohito becomes emperor of Japan.	Puccini, *Turandot*. T E Lawrence, *The Seven Pillars of Wisdom*. A A Milne, *Winnie the Pooh*. Fritz Lang, *Metropolis*.

1927	Joe Glaser, manager of the Sunset, fires Dickerson as leader and Louis takes over the band, but stays with Tate until April, when he joins Clarence Jones at the Metropolitan Theater. Armstrong, Singleton and pianist Earl Hines open their own nightclub, which flops.
1928	Hines replaces Lil in the Hot Five recording band; they record 'West End Blues' and 'Weather Bird'. Gives up the cornet for the trumpet. Rejoins Dickerson at the newly opened Savoy Ballroom.
1929	Records 'Knockin' a Jug' with a mixed-race band and 'Mahogany Hall Stomp' with the Luis Russell band. In May the Dickerson band goes on tour, ending in a four-month residency at Connie's Inn in New York, then breaks up. Appears in the Broadway revue 'Hot Chocolates'. Tommy Rockwell becomes his manager.
1930	After touring with Russell and later the Mills Blue Rhythm Band, Armstrong goes to Los Angeles and fronts the band at the New Cotton Club. Records with Jimmie Rodgers, 'the Father of Country Music'. Arrested in November for smoking marijuana, but released.
1931	In March Armstrong and Collins leave California and go to a Chicago nightclub, the Showboat, with a new band. Nationwide tour, including three months in New Orleans.
1932	Returns to Chicago and breaks up the band. Leaves NY on the SS *Majestic*, reaching Plymouth, England on 14 July. Returns to New York in November to join the cast of 'Connie's Hot Chocolates of 1932'.
1933	Forms a new band in Chicago for a tour, disbanding in June. Plays in Pittsburgh then sails for England again, opening in London on 5 August. Touring and holidaying, he spends the following year in Europe, much of it in Paris with Alpha.
1935	Returns to United States and makes Joe Glaser his manager. Forms a new band for touring, but breaks it up in September and takes the Luis Russell band with him for a residency at Connie's Inn in New York.
1936	Appears in the film 'Pennies from Heaven'. Publishes autobiography, *Swing That Music* and records a song of the same name.

1927	Joseph Stalin comes to power.	Martin Heidegger, *Being and Time.*
	Charles Lindbergh flies across Atlantic.	Virginia Woolf, *To the Lighthouse.*
		BBC public radio launched.

1928	Kellogg-Briand Pact for Peace.	Maurice Ravel, *Boléro.*
	Alexander Fleming discovers penicillin.	Kurt Weill, *The Threepenny Opera.*
		D H Lawrence, *Lady Chatterley's Lover.*
		Walt Disney, *Steamboat Willie.*

1929	Lateran Treaty.	Robert Graves, *Good-bye to All That.*
	Yugoslavia under kings of Serbia.	Ernest Hemingway, *A Farewell to Arms.*
	In US, Wall Street crash, Great Depression begins.	
	Young Plan for Germany.	

1930	Mahatma Gandhi leads Salt March in India.	W H Auden, *Poems.*
	Frank Whittle patents turbo-jet engine.	T S Eliot, 'Ash Wednesday'.
	Pluto discovered.	William Faulkner, *As I Lay Dying.*
		Evelyn Waugh, *Vile Bodies.*

1931	King Alfonso XIII flees; Spanish republic formed.	*City Lights,* with Charlie Chaplin.
	In US, Al Capone sentenced to 11 years for tax evasion.	
	Building of Empire State Building completed in New York.	

| 1932 | First autobahn opened, between Cologne and Bonn. | Aldous Huxley, *Brave New World.* |
| | | Jules Romains, *Les hommes de bonne volonté.* |

1933	Nazi Party wins German elections.	André Malraux, *La condition humaine.*
	Adolf Hitler appointed chancellor.	Gertrude Stein, *The Autobiography of Alice B Toklas.*
	F D Roosevelt president in US; launches New Deal.	

1935	In Germany, Nuremberg Laws enacted.	George Gershwin, *Porgy and Bess.*
	Philippines becomes self-governing.	Christopher Isherwood, *Mr Norris Changes Trains.*
	Italy invades Ethiopia.	Marx Brothers, *A Night at the Opera.*

| 1936 | Germany occupies Rhineland. | Prokofiev, *Peter and the Wolf.* |
| | Edward VIII abdicates throne in Britain; George VI becomes king. | A J Ayer, *Language, Truth and Logic.* |

1937   Becomes the first African-American to host a national network radio pro-
        gramme. Between touring makes two films, 'Artists and Models' and
        'Everyday's a Holiday', with Mae West.

1938   Continued touring takes him to New Orleans. Divorces Lil and marries
        Alpha in Houston in October.

1939   A year on tour ends in October with a New York residency at the Cotton
        Club, where he meets the chorus-girl Lucille Wilson. Plays Bottom on
        Broadway in 'Swingin' the Dream', based on Shakespeare, but the show
        closes after 16 days.

1940–1 Saxophonist Joe Garland takes over as musical director from Luis Russell as
        the band's tours continue.

1942–3 American Federation of Musicians imposes recording ban on 1 August
        1942. Armstrong divorces Alpha, marries Lucille on 12 October.

1944–5 On stage at the Metropolitan Opera House with other *Esquire* poll-winners
        in January 1944. In the second *Esquire* concert the following year he leads a
        small pick-up group in New Orleans for a coast-to-coast radio hook-up with
        Duke Ellington in Los Angeles and Benny Goodman in New York.

	Anti-Comintern Pact between Japan and Germany. Spanish Civil War (until 1939).	BBC public television founded.
1937	Arab-Jewish conflict in Palestine. Japan invades China. In US, Du Pont patents nylon.	Jean-Paul Sartre, *La Nausée*. John Steinbeck, *Of Mice and Men*. Picasso, *Guernica*.
1938	In Soviet Union, trial of Nikolai Bukharin and other political leaders. Kristallnacht: in Germany, Jewish houses, synagogues and schools are burnt down, and shops looted. Austrian Anschluss with Germany. Munich Crisis. Czechoslovakia cedes Sudetenland. In east and west Africa, Pan-Africanist movement gains strength.	Elizabeth Bowen, *The Death of the Heart*. Graham Greene, *Brighton Rock*. Evelyn Waugh, *Scoop*. Disney, *Snow White and the Seven Dwarfs*.
1939	Stalin and Hitler sign non-aggression pact. 1 September: Germany invades Poland. Britain and France declare war on Germany.	Steinbeck, *The Grapes of Wrath*. John Ford, *Stagecoach* with John Wayne. David O Selznick, *Gone with the Wind* with Vivien Leigh and Clark Gable.
1941	Germany occupies France, Belgium, the Netherlands, Norway and Denmark. In Britain, Winston Churchill becomes PM. Battle of Britain begins. Leon Trotsky assassinated in Mexico.	Hemingway, *For Whom the Bell Tolls*. Chaplin, *The Great Dictator*. Disney, *Fantasia*.
1943	Singapore surrenders. Battle of Guadalcanal. US relocates and interns 110,000 Japanese-Americans.	Albert Camus, *L'Etranger*. Jean Anouilh, *Antigone*. *Casablanca* with Ingrid Bergman and Humphrey Bogart.
1945	Normandy invasion. Paris is liberated. Arnhem disaster. Civil war in Greece.	Jorge Luis Borges, *Fictions*. Eisenstein, *Ivan the Terrible*. Laurence Olivier, *Henry V*.

1946	10 January, first studio recording with Ellington and other *Esquire* poll-winners on 'Long Long Journey'. Records with Ella Fitzgerald and Billie Holiday. Louis and Billie appear together in Hollywood feature, 'New Orleans'.
1947	Performances at at Carnegie Hall on 8 February and Town Hall in May. Disbands big band after final engagement at Apollo Theater and opens at Billy Berg's in Hollywood on 13 August as Louis Armstrong and His All Stars, a six-piece touring band which will be the basis of his work for the rest of his life.
1948	Takes All Stars to Nice for first world's first international jazz festival. Second recording ban in US runs from 1 January to 15 December.
1949	Crowned King of the Zulus at New Orleans Mardi Gras. Appearances on Eddie Condon TV show and Bing Crosby radio show.
1950–3	In 1953 the All Stars join a revived Benny Goodman band on tour. Appears in film 'The Glenn Miller Story' with James Stewart.
1954	Records album 'Louis Armstrong plays W C Handy' and four-disc 'Musical Autobiography'. Tours Australia and Japan.
1955–6	Tours Europe, Australia and Far East. Records 'Mack the Knife' in September 1955. In May 1956 returns to Britain after 22 years' absence, then for the first time to Africa. Appears with Bing Crosby and Frank Sinatra in 'High Society' and in documentary 'Satchmo the Great'.
1957	Records with Oscar Peterson and Ella Fitzgerald. Condemns racial segregation during dispute over school access in Little Rock, Arkansas, and calls President Dwight D Eisenhower '*two-faced*'. Cancels State Department-sponsored tour to Soviet Union.

1946	Cold War begins. In Argentina, Juan Perón becomes president. In Germany, Nuremberg trials. In Italy, women enfranchised. In Britain, National Health Service founded.	Bertrand Russell, *History of Western Philosophy*. Eugene O'Neill, *The Iceman Cometh*. Jean Cocteau, *La Belle et la Bête*.
1947	Puppet Communist states in eastern Europe. India becomes independent. Chuck Yeager breaks the sounds barrier.	Tennessee Williams, *A Streetcar named Desire*. Anne Frank, *The Diary of Anne Frank*. Jean Genet, *The Maids*.
1948	Marshall Plan (until 1951). Berlin airlift. In South Africa, Apartheid legislation passed. Gandhi is assassinated.	Norman Mailer, *The Naked and the Dead*. Alan Paton, *Cry, the Beloved Country*. Vittorio De Sica, *Bicycle Thieves*.
1949	Nato formed. Mao Zedong proclaims China a People's Republic.	George Orwell, *1984*. Simone de Beauvoir, *The Second Sex*. Arthur Miller, *Death of a Salesman*.
1950	Schuman Plan. Korean War begins (until 1953). China conquers Tibet.	Eugène Ionesco, *The Bald Prima Donna*. Billy Wilder, *Sunset Boulevard*.
1954	In Egypt, Nasser becomes prime minister. In Vietnam, French surrender at Dien Bien Phu. In US, Senate censures Joseph McCarthy.	Bill Haley and the Comets, 'Rock Around the Clock'. *On the Waterfront*, with Marlon Brando.
1955	West Germany joins NATO. Warsaw Pact formed.	James Baldwin, *Notes of a Native Son*. Satyajit Ray, *Pather Panchali*. James Dean dies in a car crash.
1957	Treaty of Rome; EEC formed. Sputnik 1 launched. Ghana becomes independent.	Leonard Bernstein (music) and Stephen Sondheim (lyrics) *West Side Story*. Jack Kerouac, *On the Road*.

1958–9	Second of frequent appearances at Newport Jazz Festival. European tour ends after heart attack at Spoleto, Umbria, in June 1959, but quickly returns to work.
1960–4	Worldwide touring. Records 'Hello Dolly!' in December 1963. In hospital in March 1964, but plays Las Vegas later in the month.
1965–7	A series of successful pop records: 'Mame' (1965), 'Cabaret' (1966) and 'What a Wonderful World' (1967). Ill with pneumonia from April to June 1967.
1968	Films a scene with Barbra Streisand for the feature, 'Hello Dolly!' Season at Variety Club, Batley, near Leeds, followed by concert dates in London. Collapses and goes into Beth Israel Hospital, New York.
1969	Released from Beth Israel, but Joe Glaser, who has had a stroke, dies there on 6 June. In October, travels to London to record title song for James Bond film.
1970	The Newport Festival presents a tribute to him, at which he sings. In September, plays and sings with the All Stars in Las Vegas, and at a charity concert in London in October.
1971	TV appearances, including one with Bing Crosby in February. Makes his last recording, reading the poem 'The Night Before Christmas'. In March he and the All Stars perform for two weeks at the Waldorf Astoria Hotel in Manhattan. Has a heart attack at home and is taken to Beth Israel on 15 March. After a month in intensive care, he leaves hospital on 6 May. On 6 July, at 5.30 am, he dies in his sleep at home.

1958	Fifth French Republic; Charles De Gaulle becomes president.	Chinua Achebe, *Things Fall Apart*.

1958 — Fifth French Republic; Charles De Gaulle becomes president.
Castro leads communist revolution in Cuba.
Texas Instruments invents silicon chip.

Chinua Achebe, *Things Fall Apart*.
Boris Pasternak, *Dr Zhivago*.
J K Galbraith, *The Affluent Society*.
Claude Lévi-Strauss, *Structural Anthropology*.
Harold Pinter, *The Birthday Party*.

1960 — U2 affair.
Sharpeville Massacre in South Africa.
Congo becomes independent.
Vietnam War begins (until 1975).
Oral contraceptives marketed.

Fellini, *La Dolce Vita*.
Alfred Hitchcock, *Psycho*.

1965 — Military coup in Indonesia.
In US, Malcolm X killed.

The Beach Boys, 'California Girls'.
Joe Orton, *Loot*.
Neil Simon, *The Odd Couple*.

1968 — In US, Martin Luther King assassinated.
In US, Robert Kennedy assassinated.
In Paris, student riots.

Kubrick, *2001: A Space Odyssey*.
The Rolling Stones, *Beggar's Banquet*.

1969 — Neil Armstrong takes first moon walk.
Internet created by US Department of Defence.
Massive anti-war rallies in US.

Kenneth Clark, *Civilization*.
Mario Puzo, *The Godfather*.
Easy Rider with Dennis Hopper and Peter Fonda.

1970 — In US, first desegregated classes held in over 200 school districts in the South.
Fighting in the Golan Heights between Israel and Syria.

Simon and Garfunkel, *Bridge Over Troubled Water*.
Germaine Greer, *The Female Eunuch*.

1971 — In Uganda, Idi Amin seizes power.
Environmental organisation Greenpeace founded.
Intel introduces the microprocessor.

Benjamin Britten, *Owen Wingrave*.
Dmitri Shostakovich, *Symphony No. 15*.
Alexander Solzhenitsyn, *August 1914*.
Kubrick, *A Clockwork Orange*.

Further Listening

The golden rule when it comes to reissues of early jazz and dance music is to look for the name John R T Davies. The master sound-restorer, who is also a musician, has set the highest standards in his digital transfers, working primarily from the best available 78rpm copies in his own collection. He deals on his website (www.jazzrescue.com) with some of the problems, not all of which are recognised by more slap-dash engineers. Davies's work, and that of his disciple, Ted Kendall, appears on a number of specialist labels, some British, some foreign, but all theoretically available from specialist dealers. To begin at the beginning, the King Oliver Creole Jazz Band are on Retrieval and their near-contemporaries in New Orleans, Papa Celestin's and Sam Morgan's bands, are together on Jazz Oracle. All of Louis's sides with Fletcher Henderson are on Forte, but non-purist customers should look on Timeless for a disc on which, at Chris Barber's suggestion, John R T Davies edited two dozen Henderson sides to give more prominence to the solos and less time to the repetitive hack arrangements. The Clarence Williams Blues Fives are also on Timeless and the Bessie Smiths are appearing on Frog. The Armstrong Hot Fives and Hot Sevens, with the first big bands, are on a four-disc set from JSP, in generally better sound than a similar set produced by CBS/Legacy, the successors to OKeh, to celebrate Louis's centenary. Two more JSP CDs cover the Armstrong big bands up to 1932. The sessions led by Johnny Dodds and Lil Armstrong are together under Dodds's name as 'New Orleans Stomp' on Frog. The Luis Russell band without Louis is on Retrieval. Some of the Mills Brothers sides with Louis are included in a set of the brothers on JSP.

Now we leave the secure zone of John R T Davies, and from this point sound quality can vary from accurate to atrocious: sometimes poor copies of 78s have been transferred at the wrong speed, sometimes adequate LP recordings have been ruined by digitising. Issues come and go, labels change their names, what offends one pair of ears may be acceptable to another, and in the case of concert recordings the original sound may have been poor.

A four-CD box on Columbia, 'Portrait of the Artist as a Young Man', gives a selection from the King Oliver days up to 1934, acompanied by a valuable essay by Dan Morgenstern. Continuing through the landmarks of Louis's career, 'The Complete RCA Victor Recordings' on BMG picks up the story in the early 30s and is one of the better efforts, except that it isn't complete: when it reaches 1947 and the Town Hall concert it has only the handful of tracks that were originally released. GRP put out three CDs of their Decca 78rpm masters and gave up: the sound was open, if a little too bright so that the cymbals could give you a shock. All the 30s and 40s Deccas, with alternative takes, are on a Swedish label, Ambassador. Fans of Big Sid Catlett can find out the effect he had on Benny Goodman on the American Vintage Jazz Classics label: Goodman plays like a man possessed on 'Roll 'Em'. Louis's V-Disc sides with Teagarden are on JazzUnlimited and the *Esquire* Metropolitan Opera House concert, complete except for a handful of tracks without Louis, is on Giants of Jazz. A three-disc Verve compilation, 'Louis Armstrong: the Ultimate Collection', misses out the OKehs but otherwise charts Louis's progress from the Henderson band to the 60s pop songs through recordings for Vocalion, Decca and other labels.

The whole Town Hall concert, and it is not to be missed, is on Fresh Sound and French RCA CD, which has vanished from the catalogue: the distorted sound on the final 'Jack-Armstrong Blues' on both issues is blamed on the valves of the recording amplifier over-heating at the end of the long concert. The

Carnegie Hall concert which led up to it, with Louis sharing his time between the Ed Hall six-piece and his own big band, is on Ambassador. The second *Esquire* concert, with Armstong, Ellington and Goodman in a trans-continental ensemble on the radio, is on Flyright, along with the performance at the Winter Garden Theater in New York by a band similar to the Town Hall group.

In the All Stars era, the concert at Symphony Hall, Boston, has been on the GRP and Giants of Jazz and a splendid GRP four-disc set. 'The California Concerts' covers the 1951 Pasadena outing with Hines and Teagarden and a 1955 date at the Crescendo with Young and Kyle. The 1956 Chicago concert is on Columbia, and so is the soundtrack of the movie 'Satchmo the Great', including recordings from the visit to the Gold Coast. Concerts by later line-ups surface from time to time: the EmArcy Gitanes label has two volumes from 1965, with Tyree Glenn and Eddie Shu, in its Jazz in Paris series. Of the studio recordings with the All Stars, the Musical Autobiography is on Jazz Ultimate and on Verve. The outstanding W C Handy album and the Fats Waller follow-up are on Columbia, but beware of the first CD issues from the 1980s, which use alternative takes: later versions have the takes originally issued. The 'Mack the Knife' duet and rehearsal with Lotte Lenya are on a Sony Classical compilation, 'Lenya Sings Weill'. Different numbers from a 1968 BBC-TV recording of the last All Stars line-up have been available on Brunswick, Moon and Milan CDs.

The main post-war vocal records are on Verve: 'Louis and the Angels', '. . . and the Good Book', 'Satchmo in Style', 'Satchmo Serenade', and the sides with Ella Fitzgerald and Oscar Peterson. Broadcasts with Bing Crosby are on Jasmine under the title 'Fun with Bing and Louis'; their Verve studio album is disappointing.

The 'Great Summit' with Duke Ellington has been reissued by Roulette with master takes on one CD and the fascinating rehearsal and alternative takes on another. The sessions with the Dukes of Dixieland have been available intermittently from Blue Moon.

Much of Armstrong's studio output from the beginning into the 1950s is issued in France on the Classics label, with alternative takes gathered up in separate issues on its sister label, Neatwork. Sound quality can vary widely, depending on the source of the transfers, but there is no doubt that Classics is doing a worthwhile job, even if it still cannot spell 'chronological', preferring 'chronogical'.

Picture Sources

The author and publishers wish to express their thanks to the following sources of illustrative material and/or permission to reproduce it. They will make proper acknowledgements in future editions in the event that any omissions have occurred.

The Bridgeman Art Collection: page vi; William P Gottlieb: frontispeace, pp. 67, 81, 86/87, 90,124; Charles Peterson: page 83; page 108 is courtesy of Russ Phillips; Photo12.com: cover; Redferns Music Pictures: pp. 15, 28, 60, 78, 84, 98; Ann Ronan: pp. 3, 8, 20, 32, 52; Topfoto: pp. 44, 52, 76, 96, 114, 116, 119, 130, 135.

Index